Material written by Gospel Broadcasting Network (GBN)

Cover design and book layout by Rob Baker

Physical distribution provided by World Video Bible School (WVBS)

ISBN: 978-160063-188-7

Gospel Broadcasting Network
8900 Germantown Rd.
Olive Branch, MS 38654

Website: https://gbntv.org
https://wvbs.org

This material is produced by GBN which is fully supported by contributions from individuals and congregations of the churches of Christ. If you are a member of the churches of Christ and would like to become a monthly supporter, go to GBNTV.org/donate.

As GBN does not sell any products or resources, WVBS has agreed to distribute this book for us.

Follow this QR Code to make a Donation

ANSWERING THE ERROR

DEVOTIONAL WORKBOOK

THE INTENT OF THIS CLASS

Jesus Christ's instruction in the Great Commission of Matthew 28:19-20 was to "Go therefore and make disciples of all the nations, baptizing them in the name of the Father and of the Son and of the Holy Spirit, teaching them to observe all things that I have commanded you; and lo, I am with you always, even to the end of the age."

As we fulfill this mission, there will be many false teachers who will "come to you in sheep's clothing, but inwardly they are ravenous wolves" Matthew 7:15. The problem with false teachers is that many times, they don't look like false teachers. As Jesus said, they come in sheep's clothing. They look outwardly to be sheep. Inwardly, not outwardly, they are ravenous wolves. The only way to know whether someone is a false teacher or not, is to listen to what they say.

Answering The Error is a TV program produced by the Gospel Broadcasting Network and this curriculum has been adapted to use those programs in a Bible class setting. *Answering The Error* started when a young man from our congregation's youth group asked a question about a video from a denominational group which focused on "Why Someone Does Not Have to Be Baptized to Be Saved." The arguments made in the video were persuasive to him as they can be to someone who has not heard them before or studied them. He shared the video with Don Blackwell and me. As Don and I watched the video, we realized these were not new arguments, but the ones we heard weekly at the Gospel Broadcasting Network. Don and I discussed and decided to do a program at GBN where we would review these videos by allowing these teachers to make their arguments for themselves and then we would step in and respond.

We hope these lessons will be used as a training tool for members of the churches of Christ to hear these arguments and how they can be answered. Many times in sermons, we make false teachers' arguments for them, and we do a very poor job. We don't make their arguments as convincing as they make them because we fear if we do, we might trick someone. However, this poses a real problem whenever a member of the church has a discussion with someone in the world who makes the false arguments persuasively. With the rise in teaching videos and articles on the internet and social media, many Christians are confused by the arguments being made on certain topics. Hopefully these lessons can help combat that false teaching.

We hoped this approach would allow members of the church to see these persuasive arguments in a safe environment. Then we would have the opportunity to respond in front of the members of the church.

The next time they heard these arguments in person, they would not be as shocked or confused, but rather they would remember that those arguments have an answer. Even if they cannot remember the exact book, chapter, and verse to respond, they know there is a resource they can go back to for those answers.

As Don starts out many episodes, we want to be clear that each of the videos that we have reviewed on Answering the Error have been submitted to us by viewers. Each time we select a video, we reach out directly to those people and organizations who have produced the videos and we always offer to have a private conversation with them about the videos they have put out first. We explain our disagreement with them based off Scripture and our concern for their souls. Sometimes they respond and we have dialogue and sometimes they do not respond.

In these lessons, we will be examining these different videos in the light of The Bible. We want to say at the very beginning (as we do in our video lessons) that it is not our intention to be combative and we are not trying to be ugly toward anyone. Our intention is simply to teach The Truth.

1 John 4:1 says that we are to "test the spirits whether they are of God because

many false prophets have gone out into the world."

In John 8:32, Jesus said "and ye shall know the truth and the truth shall make you free."

We are not trying to pick a fight with anyone. We are concerned not only about the souls of the people watching this program, but also about the souls of the people that are presenting this material in these videos.

We hope that as you go through this class that you will learn how to answer these religious errors more perfectly. Our greatest hope is that after you learn these things, that you will go out into the world and teach people the Truth in love (Eph. 4:15) and that the way you present this evidence will be consistent with Colossians 4:6.

Col. 4:6 "*Let* your speech always *be* with grace, seasoned with salt, that you may know how you ought to answer each one."

SPECIAL NOTE

Not every single statement that these men will make in their videos are wrong. In some videos, it was minutes in before they said anything that we disagreed with. We should never disagree with someone on everything, just because we disagree with them on somethings. The Bible is the source of Truth and whether we agree with a statement should always coincide with whether that statements agrees with the totality of Bible teaching. If we stick to The Bible then we will agree with what others say which is True and disagree with what they say which is not True (John 17:17, Acts 17:11).

THE CONTENT OF THE CLASS

In this class, the following videos will be covered. This book contains only 13 lessons, one quarter worth of material. Following Quarters material will be in separate books (see back of book for listing of other books).

1. Do I Have to Be Baptized to Be Saved? (4 Class Periods)

2. Once Saved, Always Saved? (2 Class Periods)

3. Why Do Catholic's Baptize Infants? (2 Class Periods)

4. Why Do I Have to Confess My Sins to a Priest? (2 Class Periods)

5. The Sinner's Prayer? (2 Class Periods)

Many of these videos are around 28 minutes long. Episodes 1, 9, and 11 are exceptions to that rule and are around 58 minutes long. Each class period will cover around 15 minutes of video, and 30 minutes of discussion. The above episodes show you how many class periods each lesson will take.

Elders or teachers, may choose to pick certain lessons they feel their congregation needs instruction on the most. These lessons are independent of each other and thus the teacher could skip certain lessons if they wanted to.

Page one contains teacher instructions that will help explain what we believe is the best process to teach through this content.

TABLE OF CONTENTS

HOW TO USE THE MATERIAL **1**

SPECIAL NOTES TO TEACHERS **2**

LESSON 1:   DO I HAVE TO BE BAPTIZED
TO BE SAVED? **5**

LESSON 2:   DO I HAVE TO BE BAPTIZED
TO BE SAVED? **13**

LESSON 3:   DO I HAVE TO BE BAPTIZED
TO BE SAVED? **19**

LESSON 4:   DO I HAVE TO BE BAPTIZED
TO BE SAVED? **31**

LESSON 5:   ONCE SAVED, ALWAYS SAVED? **43**

LESSON 6:   ONCE SAVED, ALWAYS SAVED? **55**

LESSON 7:   WHY DO CATHOLICS
BAPTIZE INFANTS? **69**

LESSON 8:   WHY DO CATHOLICS
BAPTIZE INFANTS? **83**

LESSON 9:   WHY DO I HAVE TO CONFESS
MY SINS TO A PRIEST? **99**

LESSON 10:   WHY DO I HAVE TO CONFESS
MY SINS TO A PRIEST? **111**

LESSON 11:   THE SINNERS PRAYER? **123**

LESSON 12:   THE SINNERS PRAYER? **137**

LESSON 13:   WHAT MUST I DO TO BE SAVED? **151**

HOW TO USE THE MATERIAL

Each class will be associated with an episode of *Answering The Error*. The best way to view the material will be to have a TV that is connected to the internet. You can also use a computer connected to the internet with an HDMI cable connected to your TV. You also can use AirPlay and other features that do the same thing. If you are in an area that does not have internet access, you can download all the episodes of Answering The Error at GBNTV.org.

Each lesson will have a QR code at the top of the lesson. This will be a link to a page on GBN's website for that lesson. The segments will be separated out into their own shorter videos so you will play one clip at a time. The timestamps for each video segment are also present in the book. These are only needed if you are not using the QR code at the top of each lesson. These timestamps are for those who do not have internet access at the time of teaching and are using previously downloaded episodes in their entirety. Also at the end of the book, we have added the QR codes for each lesson so that the teacher can tear out or print copies of the QR codes. These can then be posted in the class on the wall or table so students can access the lessons as well if they want to.

Each lesson will give the teacher timestamps as to when to start and stop the video. These timestamps will give the teacher a small selection of the video to play for the class. The teacher will start and then stop the video at those time stamps.

The teacher will then ask the class what arguments were made? For instance, in episode 1 "Do I Have to Be Baptized to Be Saved?", the false teacher makes the statement "we do not have to be baptized because Abraham was not baptized." After watching the video clip, the teacher will be prompted to ask the class to describe the arguments made. Then the student might say "He said Abraham wasn't baptized so we do not have to be."

The teacher will have in their teacher book the arguments the false teacher makes. This will help the teacher to tell the students the arguments if the students do not speak up. After the students tell what arguments were made, the teacher will ask the students to explain how they would answer that argument themselves. After a period of discussion where the students are allowed to give their answers, the teacher will play Don and Aaron's response in the video. After Don and Aaron's response, the teacher will stop the video again and allow for the students to discuss the answers Don and Aaron gave. The students may think the answers were good or maybe not. Let the students discuss which were their favorite arguments, which were their least. The goal is to get them talking so the material sinks into their minds.

The teacher can also write down any additional questions the students might have. I would recommend saving this portion until the end of the sessions as many questions may

be addressed later in the video. Most of the videos are 30 minutes long which will likely last 2 class periods. The hour-long episodes will take likely 4 class periods to complete.

SPECIAL NOTE TO TEACHERS:

It is possible that during this course, some students may ask questions like:

"Why are we doing this? This class just feels like we are picking on others' beliefs. Who are we to judge other people? These videos feel mean."

One thing to remember is that it's possible these students have never heard or seen others standing up to religious error so as a teacher, we need to be patient with them and hear them out, as opposed to getting upset that they are questioning why. These verses below can be used as a first study before beginning this curriculum if needed to set the stage for the rest of the class.

These are some key Scriptures to remember when responding. They have been designed below in the form of questions that you can ask if any students are not fans of this method of reviewing material.

1. Do you all think heaven and hell are real?
   a. Yes, Matthew 10:28, 13:50

2. Do you think all people are going to go to one or the other?
   a. Yes, John 5:28-29

3. Do you think where they end up is for eternity?
   a. Yes, Matthew 25:46, 2 Thess. 1:9

4. Do you think Jesus told the Truth in John 12:48 when He said we would be judged by His Words?
   a. Yes

5. Do you think that if we truly love people we should tell them The Truth? Or should we just avoid conflict and confrontation because we might upset them?
   a. Matthew 10:34-36

6. If a doctor knew you had cancer, would you want him to tell you? Or just let you go on with your life because that news might upset you?
   a. Mark 9:43

7. Do you think sin which causes spiritual death is worse than cancer which only causes physical death?
   a. Rom. 6:23

8. If it is loving for a doctor to tell a cancer patient they have cancer, wouldn't it be

more loving to tell someone of their potential spiritual death?

a. Gal. 4:1   b. Matthew 5:43-48

If we truly believe in heaven and hell and what Jesus said about them, then true love is being willing to tell people about what The Bible teaches even when it is uncomfortable and has the potential to cause an argument.

We should <u>always</u> conduct these conversations with love and grace in our speech (Col. 4:6, Eph. 4:15). The goal is to win the soul, not just to win the argument (Prov. 11:30).

LESSON: 1

EP. 1—DO I HAVE TO BE BAPTIZED TO BE SAVED?

Play Section 1 Intro/Arguments - 0:00-3:06

CLASS QUESTION: What argument/arguments did he make?

ARGUMENTS

1. "Why would you not want to be baptized if you have a relationship with Jesus Christ?"

CLASS QUESTION: How would you answer this?

CLASS QUESTION: Did he make any other arguments?

- **HINT:** He said people who have not been baptized take the Lord's Supper. In Scripture, the instruction to take the Lord's Supper is given to Christians alone (1 Cor. 11:23ff).

AFTER DISCUSSION PLAY THE NEXT VIDEO SECTION.

Play Section 1 Response - 3:07-5:58

CLASS QUESTION: Did you agree with their response?

CLASS QUESTION: Would you have made any other arguments?

- Have the class discuss the response.

TEACHERS NOTES FOR DISCUSSION

2. Sin separates us from God – Is. 59:1-2

3. A person cannot have a relationship or be reconciled to God until they have their sins are forgiven (Col. 1:20).

4. Sins are forgiven by the blood of Christ (Revelation 1:5) at the point of baptism (Acts 22:16).

5. One is baptized into the death of Christ and raised to new life (a new relationship) in baptism (Romans 6:3-4).

6. The Roman Christians were set free from their sins at the point of their baptism by contacting the blood of Christ (Romans 6:17-18).

AFTER DISCUSSION ENDS, MOVE ON TO SECTION 2.

Play Section 2 Arguments - 5:58-6:08

CLASS QUESTION: What argument/arguments did he make?

ARGUMENTS

1. "If anyone says that you have to do anything other

than acknowledge my sin and trust in God's provision for my sin, they are trifling with the Gospel."

CLASS QUESTION: What does he mean by this?

- **HINT**: He means all you have to do to be saved is realize we have sin and then trust or believe in Christ.

CLASS DISCUSSION: How would you answer this?

AFTER DISCUSSION ENDS, PLAY DON AND AARON'S RESPONSE.

Play Section 2 Response - 6:09-10:24

CLASS QUESTION: Did you agree with their response?

CLASS QUESTION: Would you have made any other arguments?

- Have the class discuss the response.

TEACHERS NOTES FOR DISCUSSION

1. "Does a Christian have to do anything other than admit sin?"
   - This man just said you don't have to do anything to be saved
2. Is this what Jesus said?
   - Acts 9:6 Saul asks Jesus this question.
     a. "Lord, what do you want me to do?" Acts 9:6

7

    b. Why didn't Jesus say "Nothing"?

    c. Jesus said "Arise and go into the city and you will be told what you must do" Acts 9:6, Acts 22:10

- What was Paul told to do by a man sent by God?

    a. Acts 22:16 "And now why are you waiting? Arise and be baptized, and wash away your sins, calling on the name of the Lord."

3. Is this what the angel sent from God said?

- In Acts 10:6, Cornelius was told to seek out the apostle Peter for "He is lodging with Simon, a tanner, whose house is by the sea. He will tell you what you must do."

4. Is this what the Holy Spirit Inspired apostle Peter himself taught?

- On the day of Pentecost, religious people heard preaching about the crucifixion of Christ and were pricked in the heart (Acts 2:21-36). They asked Peter "what shall we do?" (Acts 2:37).

5. Did Peter respond in Acts 2:38 with "you don't have to do anything?"

- No, "Then Peter said to them, "Repent, and let every one of you be baptized in the name of Jesus Christ for the re-

mission of sins; and you shall receive the gift of the Holy Spirit." Acts 2:38

6. If the idea "that if you say you have to do anything is trifling with the Gospel, then why did Peter, Paul, God's angel, The Holy Spirit, and Jesus Himself not give that answer? They all said there is something you must do.

Additional Bible Passages for class study and discussion

- Matthew 7:21, 25:21, 31
- Acts 10:35
- 1 John 2:17, 3:7

CLASS QUESTION: Can something be a gift but still have terms to accept the Gift?

- **HINT:** Read and Discuss Joshua 6:2-3, Hebrews 11:30

- Notice God gave them a city, yet gave them requirements of things they had to do to obtain the city.

- Hebrews 11:30 says "by faith the walls of Jericho fell". This shows faith is not just belief, but obedient trust. Without obedience it is not true Biblical saving faith." (Heb.5:9)

Play Section 3 Arguments from 10:25-12:02

CLASS QUESTION: What was his argument here?

9

ARGUMENTS

1. First, he states "Eph. 2:8-10 says that we are saved by grace through faith not of works."

2. Then, he states "if we can show anyone who goes to heaven without being baptized then know that you don't have to be baptized to be saved."

   - His example is Abraham

   - He states that Abraham "didn't do anything except believe" and he reads Romans 4:2-3.

CLASS QUESTION: How would you answer this statement?

- **HINT:** Romans 4:2-3 quotes Genesis 15:6. Is Genesis 15:6 where Abraham's relationship started with God?

- **HINT:** What covenant did Abraham live under? Patriarchal Covenant

- **HINT:** When was the command to be baptized in the name of the Father, Son, and Holy Spirit given? (Aka The Great Commision). Abraham lived 2000 years before the great commission was given.

AFTER DISCUSSION ENDS, PLAY NEXT SECTION.

Play Section 3 Responses from 12:02-17:21

CLASS QUESTION: Did you agree with their response?

CLASS QUESTION: Would you have made any other arguments?

- Have the class discuss the response.

TEACHERS NOTES FOR DISCUSSION

1. "Abraham didn't do anything" and cites Romans 4:2-3

   - Romans 4:2-3 quotes Genesis 15:6
   - Abraham's initial relationship with God started in Genesis 12:1ff

     a. God instructed Abraham to leave his land and told him that if he did "all the families of the earth shall be blessed" Gen. 12:3

     b. Gen. 22:18 later tells us that "in your seed all the nations of the earth shall be blessed, because you have obeyed My voice."

     c. Hebrews 11:8 also tells us that "by faith Abraham obeyed when he was called to go out to the place which he would receive as an inheritance. And he went out, not knowing where he was going."

   - Compare Romans 4:2-3 and James 2:21

     a. Romans 4:2-3 says "Abraham was justified by works"

     b. James 2:21 says "a man is not justified by works"

     c. Both of these passages quote

Genesis 15:6

d. Is this a contradiction?

    i. No, there are different types of works being discussed

    ii. Romans 4 is discussing works of the Law of Moses (Romans 3:20,28), in context circumcision (Romans 4:9-12)

    iii. James 2 is speaking of works of obedience that make faith complete or "perfect"

2. What covenant did Abraham live under?

- Patriarchy. Those under patriarchy where never told to be baptized, but they were told to offer sacrifices. They had to be obedient under the system they lived under.

- We live under the Christian covenant which started in Acts 2. The commands given in the Great Commission outlined baptism as a part of salvation under the Christian covenant. That's what we live under today.

ANSWERING
THE
ERROR

LESSON: **2**

EP. 1—DO I HAVE TO BE BAPTIZED TO BE SAVED?

Play Section 4 Argument - 17:22-17:35

CLASS QUESTION: What argument/arguments did he make?

ARGUMENTS

1. "People were saved the same way in the Old Testament and the New."

CLASS QUESTION: How would you answer this argument?

Play Section 4 Response - 17:35-22:16

CLASS QUESTION: Did you agree with their response?

CLASS QUESTION: Would you have made any other arguments?

- Have the class discuss the response.

13

TEACHERS NOTES FOR DISCUSSION

1. Argument "People were saved differently in OT than New Testament"
   - All people are saved by the blood of Jesus
   - All people are saved by faith in God
   - BUT, throughout time, people have had to express that faith in different ways.

     a. <u>Patriarchy</u> – Saving faith under the Patriarchal System was expressed by offering the animal sacrifices by the head of the family (Job 1:5, Heb. 11:4,7-9)

     b. <u>Law of Moses</u> – Saving faith was expressed through obedience to the Law of Moses. People did not have to be perfect, they just had to be faithful.

     c. <u>Christianity</u>- Saving faith is expressed through obedience to God's commands in the New Testament, no longer the Law of Moses (Heb. 8:13).

     d. We must rightly divide God's Word (2 Timothy 2:15) and one of the basic points of understanding the Bible is understanding the different covenants that have existed.

2. The argument "Abraham wasn't baptized therefore I don't have to be baptized" is similar to the more common

14

argument "the thief on the cross wasn't baptized"

- Luke 23:43 And Jesus said to him, "Assuredly, I say to you, today you will be with Me in Paradise."

- Luke 24:46-47 Then He said to them, "Thus it is written, and thus it was necessary for the Christ to suffer and to rise from the dead the third day, and that repentance and remission of sins should be preached in His name to all nations, beginning at Jerusalem."

- That New Covenant came into force in Acts 2 on the Day of Pentecost.

- A similar analogy would be, "Since George Washington didn't have to pay federal income tax, I don't have to pay federal income tax"

  a. George Washington lived under different laws than we do today, thus it would not have been breaking the law for him to not pay federal income tax, but if we tried that today, we would end up fined or possible in jail.

Play Section 5 Argument – 22:27-23:03

CLASS QUESTION: What argument/arguments did he make?

ARGUMENTS

1. He says "Romans says we are justified by faith, not

by what we do"

2. He then quotes Titus 3:5, tries to say baptism is a work that we do, therefore it's not required"

CLASS QUESTION: How would you answer this argument?

Play Section 5 Response 23:03-31:10

CLASS QUESTION: Did you agree with their response?

CLASS QUESTION: Would you have made any other arguments?

- Have the class discuss the response.

TEACHERS NOTES FOR DISCUSSION

1. He says "Romans says we are justified by faith, not by what we do"

   - Paul never says this. Paul does quote from the minor prophet Habakkuk 2:4 "the just shall live by faith" in Romans 1:17 to show that the gospel is not only for the puffed up Jews, but also for the Gentiles.

   - We are going to be judged by Jesus's Words John 12:48

   - Paul asked Jesus what to do and Jesus told Paul in Acts 9:6 and Acts 22:10 there was something he must/was appointed for him to do.

16

- What was that? Acts 22:16 Ananias told him to "arise, be baptized, and wash away your sins, calling on the name of the Lord."
- James 2:21-24
  a. "Was not Abraham our father justified by works when he offered Isaac his son on the altar? Do you see that faith was working together with his works, and by works faith was made perfect? And the Scripture was fulfilled which says, "Abraham believed God, and it was accounted to him for righteousness." And he was called the friend of God. You see then that a man is justified by works, and not by faith only."

  b. James 2:21-24 shows we are not justified by faith/belief alone, apart from obedience to God's commands.
- Galatians 2:16 shows us that we are saved by faith, the gospel system of faith, not by works of the Law of Moses
  a. Is baptism a work of the law of Moses? Or a part of Faith?

  b. Galatians 3:23-27 teaches that those who are sons of God by faith (the system of faith/the gospel) are those who have been baptized into Christ. Baptism is a part of the system of faith, the gospel.

2. His second argument was from Titus 3:5

- He said baptism was a work of righteousness
- That is not what Titus 3:5 is saying. Titus 3:5 is saying we will never earn salvation by doing any works, but that we are saved by God's Mercy and Grace.
- Then the Bible says "He saved us (Christians) by the washing of regeneration and renewal of the Holy Spirit."
    a. That is baptism. When a person is baptized, they are reborn, born again (John 3:3-5), regenerated by God by the blood of Christ which washes away our sins.
- See the Chart on the right and examine the parallel passages of Titus 3:5, Ephesians 5:26, and John 3:3-5.

TITUS 3:5 EXPLAINED BY EXAMINING OTHER PASSAGES

TITUS 3:5	SAVED	2 THINGS	- Washing of Water - Renewing of the Holy Spirit
EPH. 5:26	CLEANSED	2 THINGS	- Washing of Water - The Word
JOHN 3:5	ENTER KINGDOM	2 THINGS	- Born of the Water - Born of the Spirit

LESSON: **3**

EP. 1—DO I HAVE TO BE BAPTIZED TO BE SAVED?

Play Section 6 Argument – 31:10-31:20

CLASS QUESTION: What argument/arguments did he make?

ARGUMENTS

1. "Romans 8:1 says 'there is now no condemnation to those who are in Christ Jesus.' It doesn't say 'for those who are in Christ Jesus and get baptized.'"

CLASS QUESTION: How would you answer this argument?

Play Section 6 Response – 31:20-32:58

CLASS QUESTION: Did you agree with their response?

CLASS QUESTION: Would you have made any other arguments?

- Have the class discuss the response.

TEACHERS NOTES FOR DISCUSSION

1. The letter of Romans is written to the saints/Christians in Rome (Romans 1:7)

   - How did they get into Christ?

     a. Rom. 6:1-4 "What shall we say then? Shall we continue in sin that grace may abound? Certainly not! How shall we who died to sin live any longer in it? <u>Or do you not know that as many of us as were baptized into Christ Jesus were baptized into His death?</u> Therefore we were buried with Him through baptism into death, that just as Christ was raised from the dead by the glory of the Father, even so we also should walk in newness of life."

     b. Consistent with Galatians 3:26-27 also which says "For you are all sons of God through faith in Christ Jesus. For as many of you as were baptized into Christ have put on Christ."

     c. Romans 6:17-18

     d. "But God be thanked, that ye were the servants of sin, but ye have obeyed from the heart that form of doctrine which was delivered you. Being then made free from sin, ye became the servants of righteousness."

CLASS DISCUSSION: Did you agree/like their arguments? Are there other passages you would have used?

Play Section 7 Argument – 32:58-33:08

CLASS QUESTION: What argument/arguments did he make?

ARGUMENTS

1. "Romans 5:1 says we are justified by faith."

2. **HINT:** He is implying that we are justified by belief alone before and without baptism.

CLASS QUESTION: How would you answer this argument?

Play Section 7 Response -33:09-35:47

CLASS QUESTION: Did you agree with their response?

CLASS QUESTION: Would you have made any other arguments?

- Have the class discuss the response.

TEACHERS NOTES FOR DISCUSSION

1. He stated that we are justified by faith Romans 5:1.

2. Is that true? Absolutely. The question is not whether we are. The Bible says we are. The question is HOW are we justi-

21

fied by faith?

- Over and over he takes a verse that says faith and assumes it means faith only or belief alone
- The Bible uses faith in many ways

a. Faith can be...

    i. a condition among other conditions as in Mark 16:16 he that believes (has faith) and it baptized shall be saved.

    ii. The System of Faith the Gospel as we can see in Jude 3 and Galatians 1:23, 3:24-27.

    iii. A personal belief about a matter of opinion as Romans 14:22 which says "Do you have faith, keep it to yourself." This is obviously not talking about our belief in Christ as it would contradict the Great Commission.

3. He makes the assertion that as soon as you believe you are saved. So what if there were people in Scripture who believed, but were not saved immediately?

- John 12:42 "Nevertheless even among the rulers many believed in Him, but because of the Pharisees they did not confess Him, lest they should be put out of the synagogue; for they loved the praise of men more than the praise of God."
- Belief alone is not enough.

3. We believe every passage that says we are saved by faith, but that faith has to be active and obedient to save (James 2:26).

- Titus 2:11-12 says "For the grace of God that brings salvation has appeared to all men, teaching us that, denying ungodliness and worldly lusts, we should live soberly, righteously, and godly in the present age,"

- Grace appeared to all in Jesus Christ and His Teachings, but we must be instructed in those things and then act on them to be saved.

CLASS DISCUSSION: Did you agree/ like their arguments? Are there other passages you would have used?

Play Section 8 Argument – 35:47-36:11

CLASS QUESTION: What argument/arguments did he make?

ARGUMENTS

1. Paul wrote in 1 Cor. 1:17 "For Christ did not send me to baptize, but to preach the gospel, not with wisdom of words, lest the cross of Christ should be made of no effect."

2. Why would Paul write this if people had to be baptized to go to heaven?

23

CLASS QUESTION: How would you answer this argument?

Play Section 8 Response – 36:12-39:46

CLASS QUESTION: Did you agree with their response?

CLASS QUESTION: Would you have made any other arguments?

- Have the class discuss the response.

TEACHERS NOTES FOR DISCUSSION

1. Why would Paul say this?

   - First, we must always study passages in their context.

   - The background of the letter to Corinth is Acts 18. This is where we see men and women taught and baptized.

   - 1 Cor. 1:2 shows us that all of these Christians had already been baptized. There is no such thing in the New Testament as a Christian who has not already been baptized.

   - If we look at the context of 1 Corinthians 1:10-17 we see there were divisions among the church in Corinth based off who baptized them. Paul is rebuking this idea and saying that Christ is the one who was crucified for you and who baptized you is irrelevant. Then Paul says I am glad I didn't baptize

24

any of you, except a few, because then you would be dragging my name into this mess.

- Paul's primary job as an apostle was to teach, not necessarily to baptize. This is similar to how Jesus conducted Himself.

- Notice John 4:1-2 which says "Therefore, when the Lord knew that the Pharisees had heard that Jesus made and baptized more disciples than John (though Jesus Himself did not baptize, but His disciples)"

- Yet Jesus taught baptism was necessary to be saved Mark 16:16, Matthew 28:18-20.

CLASS DISCUSSION: Did you agree/ like their arguments? Are there other passages you would have used?

- If time permits, have the class read 1 Cor. 1:10-17.

Play Section 9 Argument –39:46-40:04

CLASS QUESTION: What argument/arguments did he make?

ARGUMENTS

1. He states "John 3:18 says he who does not believe in Jesus is judged. It doesn't say "he who does not believe and is not baptized will be judged"

CLASS QUESTION: How would you answer this argument?

Play Section 9 Response – 40:04-43:02

CLASS QUESTION: Did you agree with their response?

CLASS QUESTION: Would you have made any other arguments?

- Have the class discuss the response.

TEACHERS NOTES FOR DISCUSSION

1. As we stated in the last segment, context is always key.

2. The context includes John 3:3-5 where Jesus told Nicodemus a man must be born again, of water and spirit. This is a reference to baptism. As BJ Clark said to someone who told him "there is no water in John 3:16", BJ replied while keeping the context in mind and said "Mam, that's because John 3:3-5 is soaking wet."

3. Further, John 3:18 He that believeth (present participle, keeps on believing) on him is not condemned: but he that believeth not is condemned already, "

   - The promise here is conditional. If one keeps on believing, they will not be condemned. Believing in Jesus would include obeying His commandments as well.

4. Also again, in the same context, notice

John 3:36.

- The NKJV states "He who believes in the Son has everlasting life; and he who does not believe the Son shall not see life, but the wrath of God abides on him."

    a. One might be led to believe that belief or non-belief is what is the determining factor. However, while the KJV and NKJV say believe in both places, in the Greek these are two different words.

- The 1901 ASV states "He that believeth on the Son hath everlasting life; but he that obeyeth not the Son shall not see life, but the wrath of God abideth on him."

- The NASB states ""He who believes in the Son has eternal life; but he who does not obey the Son will not see life, but the wrath of God abides on him."

    a. This verse shows that belief is necessary to salvation, but disobedience will lead to condemnation. This passage could be placed next to Mark 16:16 to show a person must not only believe, but also be obedient (John 3:36) and be baptized (Mark 16:16).

    b. This chapter overall teaches that belief alone does not save, but a faith that believes and obeys all the instructions given by God.

CLASS DISCUSSION: Did you agree/ like their arguments? Are there other passages you would have used?

Play Section 10 Argument – 43:02-43:16

CLASS QUESTION: What argument/arguments did he make?

ARGUMENTS

1. He quotes "John 1:12 But as many as received Him, to them He gave the right to become children of God, to those who believe in His name:" and then states that he is giving verse, after verse, after verse" to prove his point

CLASS QUESTION: How would you answer this argument?

Play Section 10 Response – 43:16-45:01

CLASS QUESTION: Did you agree with their response?

CLASS QUESTION: Would you have made any other arguments?

- Have the class discuss the response.

TEACHERS NOTES FOR DISCUSSION

1. What does John 1:12 actually say? It does not say that those who received Him or believed in Him were automatically saved. It says those who received/ believed in Him, He gave the right to

become children of God.

- When a person becomes a resident of a new state, they do not automatically get a drivers license. They have the right to get one, but how? According to the terms and requirements the state sets out.

- So how did they become sons of God?

   a. Galatians 3:26-27 "For you are all sons of God through faith in Christ Jesus. For as many of you as were baptized into Christ have put on Christ."

2. He has given us lots of verses so far in this video, but here is the problem.

- He has not produced any verses that say a man is saved by faith alone, as in belief only, which is what he means by "faith alone".

- He has given us verses that say we must have faith and belief which we agree with, but he has not explained the passages that say a person must be baptized to be saved.

- For example, imagine a man was caught on camera stealing a TV from a store and brought before a judge. The man's lawyer says to the judge, your honor we can produce 1000 witnesses who will attest that they did not see this man steal the TV. What would the judge say? That is irrel-

evant. We would agree those 1000 witnesses didn't see the man steal the TV. What you need to do is explain the surveillance video that shows your client stealing the TV. You need to explain to us why that is not your client or the video is fake, etc.

- In like manner, what he needs to do is explain for instance why Ananias told Paul he still needed to wash his sins away in Acts 22:16, after Paul had already met Jesus, confessed Him as Lord, prayed, and fasted for 3 days (Acts 9:6-11). Paul had done everything this man would say he needed to in order to be saved, yet Ananias said he was not saved yet from his sins. Someone needs to explain this passage away instead of just saying "this verse says you have to believe". We teach that as well.

CLASS DISCUSSION: Did you agree/ like their arguments? Are there other passages you would have used?

LESSON: **4**

EP. 1—DO I HAVE TO BE BAPTIZED TO BE SAVED?

Play Section 11 Argument – 45:01-45:31

CLASS QUESTION: What argument/arguments did he make?

ARGUMENTS

1. He says there are a few people that when they ask Paul or Peter the question what must I do to be saved, that they might hear "believe and be baptized". He says that is a natural outflow of belief or faith, but if you take those verses as a prescription for what people must do, that is wrong because there are so many other verses that teach we are saved by grace alone, through faith alone, in Christ alone."

    • What is he saying here?

    • **HINT:** He is saying just because The Bible shows people asking how to be saved to apostles

31

like Peter and Paul, and those inspired apostles respond "Be baptized", that doesn't mean that is actually what all people have to do because other verses say we are saved by grace alone, thru faith alone, in Christ alone.

CLASS QUESTION: How would you answer this argument?

Play Section 11 Response – 45:32- 49:47

CLASS QUESTION: Did you agree with their response?

CLASS QUESTION: Would you have made any other arguments?

- Have the class discuss the response.

TEACHERS NOTES FOR DISCUSSION

1. He said that those verses are not pre-scriptive for all people.

   - Is that true? The Great Commission in Matthew 28:18-20 and Mark 16:15-16 both teach that the Gospel message including "he that believes and is baptized shall be saved" is for all nations and all creatures.

2. He is partially correct that some people taught those who asked how to be saved to "repent and be baptized". Who were those people?

32

- Peter Acts 2:37-38,40-41
- Paul Acts 22:16
- Jesus Acts 9:6, 22:10
- God's Angel Acts 10:6

3. It is also interesting that his claim is a person is saved first and baptized later. If that is true, then why are the letters from Romans-Revelation which are written to Christians completely absent of the command for a "saved person to be baptized". Not one time do you see that. The only conclusion is that no one was saved prior to their baptism. Otherwise, Paul never once instructed a person to do what this man says is the first thing a "saved person should do"

4. He also made a comment implying that there were only a few instances of belief and baptism, while the vast majority included grace alone, by faith alone, in Christ alone. This chart below shows that this is not the case. In fact, there is not one single Scripture in the Bible that teaches we are saved by grace alone or faith/belief alone. We are saved by Christ, but even after His Death, Burial, and Resurrection, He told the apostles that they would be inspired by the Holy Spirit to teach His Words (John 16:12-15) and the apostles frequently taught that Jesus had done his part and now believers had to do their part and respond by repenting, confessing, and being

baptized to show their faith in the work that God would do of cutting their sins away spiritually when they were baptized physically in water (Acts 2:38, Col. 2:11-12, 1 Peter 3:21).

CONVERSIONS IN THE BOOK OF ACTS

Preaching	Believing	Repented	Confession	Baptized/Saved
Pentecost (Acts 2:14ff)	**Implied** (vs. 37, 41)	**Repent** (vs. 37-38)		**Taught** (v. 38) **Baptized** (v. 41)
Samaria (Acts 8:5ff)	**Believed** (vs 12, 13)			**Baptized** (vs. 12-13, 16)
The Eunuch (Acts 8:35-39)	**Taught and Believed** (v. 37)		**Confessed** (v. 37)	**Baptized** (v. 38)
Saul (Acts 9, 22,26)	**Implied** (Acts 9:6, 22:10)	**Implied** (Acts 9:9, 11)	**Implied** (Acts 9:6, 22:10)	**Taught** (Acts 22:16) **Baptized** (Acts 9:18)
Cornelius (Acts 10-11)	**Taught** (Acts 10:43)	**Implied** (Acts 11:18)		**Commanded** (Acts 10: 47-48)
Lydia (Acts 16:13)	**Implied** (v. 14)			**Baptized** (v. 15)
The Jailer (Acts 16:31ff)	**Taught** (v. 31)			**Baptized** (v. 33)

Corinthians (Acts 18:8)	**Believed** (v. 8)			**Baptized** (v. 8)
Ephesians (Acts 19:1ff)	**Taught** (v. 4)			**Baptized** (v. 5)

CLASS DISCUSSION: Did you agree/like their arguments? Are there other passages you would have used?

Play Section 12 Argument – 49:47-50:09

CLASS QUESTION: What argument/arguments did he make?

ARGUMENTS

1. He simply quotes 1 John 5:11-12. "And this is the testimony: that God has given us eternal life, and this life is in His Son. He who has the Son has life; he who does not have the Son of God does not have life."

CLASS QUESTION: How would you answer this argument?

Play Section 12 Response – 50:09-51:32

CLASS QUESTION: Did you agree with their response?

CLASS QUESTION: Would you have made any other arguments?

- Have the class discuss the response.

35

TEACHERS NOTES FOR DISCUSSION

1. This verse is beautiful and correct obviously. The key thing to focus on in this verse is that those who have eternal life, have it because they are in Christ, the Son. That is the source of spiritual life.

   - 2 Timothy 2:10 says the same thing

     a. "Therefore I endure all things for the sake of the elect, that they also may obtain the salvation which is in Christ Jesus with eternal glory."

   - The question then should be asked "How does one get into Christ?"

     a. Romans 6:3-4

     b. One gets into Christ by being baptized into Christ

CLASS DISCUSSION: Did you agree/ like their arguments? Are there other passages you would have used?

> **Play Section 13 Argument – 51:32- 51:46**

CLASS QUESTION: What argument/arguments did he make?

ARGUMENTS

1. His words are "There is nothing in the Scripture that when you look at the revelation of God that would indicate that anything that we do, and baptism is something that we do, that would allow us to be saved"

CLASS QUESTION: How would you answer this argument?

Play Section 13 Response – 51:46-53:57

CLASS QUESTION: Did you agree with their response?

CLASS QUESTION: Would you have made any other arguments?

- Have the class discuss the response.

TEACHERS NOTES FOR DISCUSSION

1. He states there is nothing in Scripture that would indicate we must do anything to be saved?

   • Scripture teaches the exact opposite

   a. Acts 2:37 this question is asked and what is the response given in Acts 2:38? "Repent and be Baptized in the name of Jesus Christ for the forgiveness of your sins"

   b. Acts 9:6, 22:10 same question is asked to Jesus and he said there was something Paul must do or was appointed for him to do.

   c. Acts 10:6 Cornelius was told there was something he must do

   d. Matthew 7:21 says that our judgement will take into account what we have done

   i. "Not everyone who says to

Me, 'Lord, Lord,' shall enter the kingdom of heaven, but he who <u>does</u> the will of My Father in heaven."

e. Matthew 25:31-46 speaks repeatedly of those faithful people who "did something to the least of these and thus did it to Jesus" while those condemned to hell are those who "did not do it to the least of these".

2. **SIDE NOTE:** Baptism is a passive action. The person being baptized is baptized. They do not baptize themselves. Col. 2:11-12 teaches that the one who works in baptism is God when we have faith in His Word and His Promises.

CLASS DISCUSSION: Did you agree/ like their arguments? Are there other passages you would have used?

Play Section 14 Argument – 53:57-54:11

CLASS QUESTION: What argument/arguments did he make?

ARGUMENTS

1. He says that I don't know why anyone would not want to be baptized, but that it is "an assault, an affront to The Gospel to say that you must do something other than believe in Jesus to be reconciled to Him."

CLASS QUESTION: How would you answer this argument?

Play Section 14 Response – 54:11- end of video

CLASS QUESTION: Did you agree with their response?

CLASS QUESTION: Would you have made any other arguments?

- Have the class discuss the response.

TEACHERS NOTES FOR DISCUSSION

1. He would assert that the Gospel we teach is another Gospel.

2. We respectfully, would tell you that the Gospel he is teaching is not the Gospel of Jesus Christ that is taught in the New Testament

   - "I marvel that you are turning away so soon from Him who called you in the grace of Christ, to a different gospel, which is not another; but there are some who trouble you and want to pervert the gospel of Christ. But even if we, or an angel from heaven, preach any other gospel to you than what we have preached to you, let him be accursed. As we have said before, so now I say again, if anyone preaches any other gospel to you than what you have received, let him be accursed." Galatians 1:6-9

ANSWERING THE ERROR

- Just a short time later in this same epistle, Paul speaks of justification by faith in Galatians 3:24-27 and Paul teaches that the faith or Gospel of Christ includes baptism to become a son of God.

- As we have shown through this video, Jesus, Peter, Paul, and many other inspired writers delivering God's message to man have consistently given commands to obey and examples of those who asked how to be saved and they were told to do something (Acts 9:6, 22:10, 2:37, etc.)

CLASS DISCUSSION: Did you agree/ like their arguments? Are there other passages you would have used?

SUMMARY CLASS DISCUSSION

- What verses do you find are the most effective in proving that baptism is for the forgiveness of sins?

- Were you caught off guard by the way this teacher presented his material? Was it more persuasive than you expected?

- Would you have been able to answer his questions off hand without studying?

- Do you feel better prepared now to deal with these arguments when you encounter them in your day-to-day evangelistic efforts?

If you or your students have any additional questions they would like answered, they are more than welcome to email Don and Aaron at **answeringtheerror@gbntv.org**

Tell the students that they can download the Gospel Broadcasting Network App to watch more episodes of Answering The Error and the many other programs that GBN has on their app and website www.GBNTV.org.

LESSON: **5**

EP. 2—ONCE SAVED, ALWAYS SAVED?

One of the false teachings in the religious world is the idea of "Once Saved, Always Saved." Many people believe this teaching that once a person has been "saved" they cannot lose their place in Heaven. They teach this is true even if the person returns to a sinful lifestyle. In this lesson, we will breakdown the arguments made in a video by Dr. Charles Stanley, which was submitted to us by a viewer. As we always do, we reached out to Dr. Stanley and received no response. Follow along with us as we seek the scriptures to answer the question, "once you're saved, are you always saved?"

Play Section 1 Intro/Arguments – 0:00- 2:21

CLASS QUESTION: What argument/arguments did he make?

ARGUMENTS

1. In this opening part of the video he says that salvation is from God and no one else and it is only

through the death, burial, and resurrection of Jesus Christ that we can receive the forgiveness of our sins.

2. He introduces the discussion by saying that "salvation is a free gift" and "it is something that we cannot earn or deserve. This gift should make us want to serve the Lord always."

CLASS QUESTION: How would you answer this? Do you agree? Disagree?

AFTER DISCUSSION PLAY THE NEXT VIDEO SECTION.

Play Section 1 Response – 2:21-3:42

CLASS QUESTION: Did you agree with their response?

CLASS QUESTION: Would you have made any other arguments?

*   Have the class discuss the response.

TEACHERS NOTES FOR DISCUSSION

1. We agree with everything he has said so far.

2. Salvation is a gift from God that we cannot earn or deserve

   *   Rom. 6:23 "For the wages of sin is death, but the gift of God is eternal life in Christ Jesus our Lord."

   *   Eph. 2:8 "For by grace you have been

saved through faith, and that not of yourselves; it is the gift of God,"

- KJV and NKJV, ASV 1901 and ESV add free to the text, while the word for free does not seem to be in the Greek text, the idea is correct. A gift is something not earned.
- Thayer's Greek Lexicon states "gift of favor one receives without any merit"

3. It is important to note that just because salvation is a "free gift", this does not imply that there are no requirements for us to receive that gift.

- God gave requirements.
- Anything we must do?
  a. Acts 9:6 Jesus told Paul there was something he must do
  b. Acts 10:6 Cornelius told there would be something he must do
  c. Act 2:37-38 These Jews on Pentecost wanted the gift of salvation from sin asked what must we do? Told to Repent and Be Baptized to be saved

CLASS DISCUSSION: Did you agree/ like their arguments? Are there other passages you would have used?

Play Section 2 Arguments – 3:42-4:20

CLASS QUESTION: What argument/arguments did he make?

ARGUMENTS

1. What happens after a person receives this gift and then lives pretty much like everyone else?

2. Then he goes to an email that he has received, "How can a person be saved, backslide into a life of sin, and still be saved for all eternity?"

CLASS QUESTION: How would you answer this?

AFTER DISCUSSION PLAY THE NEXT VIDEO SECTION.

Play Section 2 Response – 4:20-9:15

CLASS QUESTION: Did you agree with their response?

CLASS QUESTION: Would you have made any other arguments?

- Have the class discuss the response.

TEACHERS NOTES FOR DISCUSSION

1. Neither the Old Testament nor New Testament support this idea

- The Old Testament teaches against this idea in Ezekiel 18

  a. Ezek. 18:24 – "But when a righteous man turns away from his righteousness and commits iniquity, and does according to all the abominations that the wicked *man* does, shall he live?" All the righteousness which he has done shall not be

remembered; because of the un-
faithfulness of which he is guilty and
the sin which he has committed,
because of them he shall die."

- The New Testament teaches against
  this idea as well

  a. "Brethren, if anyone among you
     wanders from the truth, and some-
     one turns him back, let him know
     that he who turns a sinner from
     the error of his way will save a soul
     from death and cover a multitude
     of sins." James 5:19-20

  b. "You have become estranged from
     Christ, you who attempt to be jus-
     tified by law; you have fallen from
     grace." Gal. 5:4

  c. "But I discipline my body and bring
     it into subjection, lest, when I have
     preached to others, I myself should
     become disqualified." 1 Corinthians
     9:27

  d. "Beware, brethren, lest there be in
     any of you an evil heart of unbelief
     in departing from the living God;"
     Heb. 3:12

  e. "Deliver such a one to Satan for
     the destruction of the flesh, that
     his spirit may be saved in the day
     of the Lord Jesus." 1 Cor. 5:5

  f. "For if, after they have escaped
     the pollutions of the world through
     the knowledge of the Lord and

Savior Jesus Christ, they are again entangled in them and overcome, the latter end is worse for them than the beginning. For it would have been better for them not to have known the way of righteousness, than having known it, to turn from the holy commandment delivered to them." 2 Peter 2:20-21

g. "Of how much worse punishment, do you suppose, will he be thought worthy who has trampled the Son of God underfoot, counted the blood of the covenant by which he was sanctified a common thing, and insulted the Spirit of grace?" Hebrews 10:29

CLASS DISCUSSION: Did you agree/ like their arguments? Are there other passages you would have used?

Play Section 3 Arguments – 9:15-9:40

CLASS QUESTION: What argument/arguments did he make?

ARGUMENTS

1. Then as proof that a saved person cannot lose his salvation, he cites John 10:28, "And I give unto them eternal life; and they shall never perish, neither shall any *man* pluck them out of my hand."

   • And he emphasizes "never perish."

- He says, "Never means never." He says "not if," not "but," not "when," Never!

CLASS QUESTION: How would you answer this?

AFTER DISCUSSION PLAY THE NEXT VIDEO SECTION.

Play Section 3 Response – 9:40- 13:26

CLASS QUESTION: Did you agree with their response?

CLASS QUESTION: Would you have made any other arguments?

- Have the class discuss the response.

TEACHERS NOTES FOR DISCUSSION

1. John 10:28 "And I give unto them eternal life; and they shall never perish, neither shall any *man* pluck them out of my hand."

   - **Context is key.** We should always look at the verses before and after a verse to make sure we don't isolate that verse from its context.

     a. John 10:27, "My sheep hear my voice, and I know them, and they follow me: **28** And I give unto them eternal life; and they shall never perish, neither shall any *man* pluck them out of my hand."

     b. First **CONTEXT**.

       i. Who does God give eternal

49

life and promise they will never perish or be plucked out of
God's hand?

ii. Verse 27 – sheep who are following him.

iii. Verse 28 – THEY shall never
perish.

iv. If a follower of Jesus faithful-
ly follows Him, they will never
perish or be taken away from
Christ, but the condition is that
they continue to follow Him.

v. 1 John 1:7, "But if we walk in the
light, as he is in the light, we
have fellowship one with another, and the blood of Jesus
Christ his Son cleanseth us from
all sin.

vi. 1 John 3:9 NASB "No one who is
born of God practices sin, because His seed abides in him;
and he cannot sin, because he
is born of God."

vii. 1 John 5:18, "We know that
whosoever is born of God sinneth not; but he that is begot-
ten of God keepeth himself,
and that wicked one toucheth
him not."

c. Jesus is saying in this context the
same thing He says in many other
places, IF you remain faithful to me,
no one can snatch you from me.

i. Romans 8:38-39 says that nothing can separate you from God, but it's not unconditional.

ii. Romans 8:13 "if you live according to the flesh you will die" and that is written to Christians

CLASS DISCUSSION: Did you agree/ like their arguments? Are there other passages you would have used?

Play Section 4 Arguments – 13:26-13:53

CLASS QUESTION: What argument/arguments did he make?

ARGUMENTS

1. He cites 2 Corinthians 5:17 which says that "if man be in Christ, he is a new creature."

2. And then John 3:3-5 where Jesus told Nicodemus that he must be born again.

3. Now, here's the argument that he makes…He says, "Once you're born, you're born."

CLASS QUESTION: How would you answer this?

AFTER DISCUSSION PLAY THE NEXT VIDEO SECTION.

Play Section 4 Response – 13:53-15:58

CLASS QUESTION: Did you agree with their response?

CLASS QUESTION: Would you have made any other arguments?

- Have the class discuss the response.

TEACHERS NOTES FOR DISCUSSION

1. The argument he is making is once you're born you can never be unborn.

   - The **point is once you're born you can die,**

      a. John 8:24 "If you do not believe that I am He, you will die in your sins."

         i. This is spoken to Jews who were in a covenant with God. They were born into that covenant. They could not be unborn out of that covenant, but they could die spiritually if they did not follow God.

         ii. In Luke 16:22-23 you have the Rich man who was Jewish, had been born into a covenant with God, who ended up lost.

            – "The rich man also died and was buried. **23** And being in torments in Hades, he lifted up his eyes and saw Abraham afar off, and Lazarus in his bosom. Luke 16:22-23"

2. 2 Peter 1:10, "Wherefore the rather, brethren, give diligence to make your calling and election sure: for **if** ye do

these things, **ye shall never fall**: [11] For so an entrance shall be ministered unto you abundantly into the everlasting kingdom of our Lord and Saviour Jesus Christ."

3. Jude 21 "keep yourselves in the love of God, waiting anxiously for the mercy of our Lord Jesus Christ to eternal life."

4. 1 Peter 1:5 "who are protected by the power of God through faith for a salvation ready to be revealed in the last time."

CLASS DISCUSSION: Did you agree/ like their arguments? Are there other passages you would have used?

LESSON: **6**

EP. 2—ONCE SAVED, ALWAYS SAVED?

Play Section 5 Arguments – 15:59- 16:16

CLASS QUESTION: What argument/arguments did he make?

ARGUMENTS

1. We're not saved because we deserve it. We're not even kept because we deserve it.

CLASS QUESTION: How would you answer this? Do you agree?

AFTER DISCUSSION PLAY THE NEXT VIDEO SECTION.

Play Section 5 Response -16:16 – 16:52

CLASS QUESTION: Did you agree with their response?

CLASS QUESTION: Would you have made any other arguments?

- Have the class discuss the response.

TEACHERS NOTES FOR DISCUSSION

1. Of course, he's right about the fact that we're not saved or kept because we deserve it, but that doesn't prove "once saved always saved?"

   - Yes we are saved by God's grace through faith (Eph. 2:8-9)
   - Titus 2:11,12 also says "the grace of God appeared bringing salvation to all men, teaching us..."
   - Hebrews 5:9, "he became the author of eternal salvation unto all them that **obey him."**
   - Once we are saved however, we must continue to "be faithful unto death" to receive our crown of life." Rev. 2:10

CLASS DISCUSSION: Did you agree/ like their arguments? Are there other passages you would have used?

Play Section 6 Arguments – 16:52-17:41

CLASS QUESTION: What argument/arguments did he make?

ARGUMENTS

1. He says that "you cannot get away with sin." He says "We're talking about a person who just goes back into a life of sin. Do they lose their salvation for all eternity? And the answer is no."

CLASS QUESTION: How would you answer this?

AFTER DISCUSSION PLAY THE NEXT VIDEO SECTION.

Play Section 6 Response – 17:41-19:15

CLASS QUESTION: Did you agree with their response?

CLASS QUESTION: Would you have made any other arguments?

- Have the class discuss the response.

TEACHERS NOTES FOR DISCUSSION

1. Is his answer different from the Bible? Yes

   - "For if, after they have escaped the pollutions of the world through the knowledge of the Lord and Savior Jesus Christ, they are again entangled in them and overcome, the latter end is worse for them than the beginning. For it would have been better for them not to have known the way of righteousness, than having known it, to turn from the holy commandment delivered to them." 2 Peter 2:20-21

   - "For it is impossible for those who were once enlightened, and have tasted the heavenly gift, and have become partakers of the Holy Spirit, and have tasted the good word of God and the powers of the age to come, if they fall away, to renew them

> again to repentance, since they cru-
> cify again for themselves the Son of
> God, and put *Him* to an open shame."
> Hebrews 6:4-6
>
> • "For if we sin willfully after we have
> received the knowledge of the truth,
> there no longer remains a sacrifice for
> sins,...29 how much worse punishment,
> do you suppose, will he be thought
> worthy who has trampled the Son of
> God underfoot, counted the blood of
> the covenant by which he was sancti-
> fied a common thing..." Heb 10:26-31

CLASS DISCUSSION: Did you agree/ like their arguments? Are there other passages you would have used?

Play Section 7 Arguments – 19:15- 20:23

CLASS QUESTION: What argument/arguments did
he make?

ARGUMENTS

1. He argues that a Christian can have guilt, "miss
   the will of God in their life," "waste away their
   life," and suffer many earthly consequences of
   living in sin, but (he says) "that's different from
   losing your salvation."

2. And he makes a distinction here between "losing
   your reward and losing your salvation."

3. And he is basing the entire argument on <u>1 Cor. 3</u>.

CLASS QUESTION: How would you answer this?

AFTER DISCUSSION PLAY THE NEXT VIDEO SECTION.

Play Section 7 Response – 20:23-22:00

CLASS QUESTION: Did you agree with their response?

CLASS QUESTION: Would you have made any other arguments?

- Have the class discuss the response.

TEACHERS NOTES FOR DISCUSSION

1. He is saying that you can lose your reward, but not your salvation and is using 1 Cor. 3 to try and teach this.

2. While 1 Cor. 3 can be confusing, I think we can see this is not what this chapter is teaching.

3. Paul begins by describing Christians as plants

   - "I planted, Apollos watered, but God was causing the growth. So then neither the one who plants nor the one who waters is anything, but God who causes the growth. Now he who plants and he who waters are one; but each will receive his own reward according to his own labor. For we are God's fellow workers; you are God's field, God's building." 1 Cor 3:6-9

   - Notice in 1 Cor. 3:9 he finishes the plant analogy and calls the Chris-

tians God's field, then transitions and call them in that same verse "God's building." In 1 Cor. 11:16 he will call the God's people His temple using similar language.

- The description as Christians being God's work or building will start in the following verse

- "According to the grace of God which was given to me, like a wise master builder I laid a foundation, and another is building on it. But each man must be careful how he builds on it. For no man can lay a foundation other than the one which is laid, which is Jesus Christ. Now if any man builds on the foundation with gold, silver, precious stones, wood, hay, straw, each man's work will become evident; for the day will show it because it is to be revealed with fire, and the fire itself will test the quality of each man's work. If any man's work which he has built on it remains, he will receive a reward. If any man's work is burned up, he will suffer loss; but he himself will be saved, yet so as through fire."
1 Cor. 3:10-15

4. In the context, Paul describes himself as a master builder and those he has converted as material being built up into a building or temple for God.

CLASS DISCUSSION: Did you agree/ like their argu-

ments? Are there other passages you would have used?

Play Section 8 Arguments – 22:00-22:26

CLASS QUESTION: What argument/arguments did he make?

ARGUMENTS

1. So the question is 'Can a person be saved by the grace of God, born again, new creation in Christ Jesus, and slip back into sin, and still go to heaven?' Yes you can!"

CLASS QUESTION: How would you answer this?

AFTER DISCUSSION PLAY THE NEXT VIDEO SECTION.

Play Section 8 Response – 22:26-23:38

CLASS QUESTION: Did you agree with their response?

CLASS QUESTION: Would you have made any other arguments?

- Have the class discuss the response.

TEACHERS NOTES FOR DISCUSSION

1. He is still arguing based off of 1 Cor. 3.

2. Some people find it hard to believe that Paul would call converts Paul's work in 1 Cor. 3:12-15. Notice however Paul uses this language more clearly in the letter elsewhere.

- 1 Cor. 9:1 "Are not you **my work** in The Lord"?

- Paul calls converts his hope, joy, and crown in 1 Thessalonians. While this language is odd to us, it is how Paul wrote.

  a. "For what is our **hope, or joy, or crown** of rejoicing? Is it not even you in the presence of our Lord Jesus Christ at His coming? For you are **our glory** and joy" (I Thessalonians 2:19-20).

3. Also, would Paul be telling you that no one could sin as to lose their salvation in 1 Cor. 3 but then later in 1 Cor. 9:27 says that he had to be careful lest he himself become a castaway?

   - 1 Cor. 9:27 "But I discipline my body and bring it into subjection, lest, when I have preached to others, I myself should become disqualified."

4. Once again, would Paul say that someone could not sin to lose their souls, but then in 1 Cor. 5 teach that the church must deliver the unfaithful brother to Satan to try and save his soul on judgement day?

   - 1 Cor. 5:5 "deliver such an one to Satan, that Spirit may be saved in the day of our Lord"

CLASS DISCUSSION: Did you agree/ like their arguments? Are there other passages you would have used?

Play Section 9 Arguments – 23:38-24:20

CLASS QUESTION: What argument/arguments did he make?

ARGUMENTS

1. In his closing statement, Mr. Stanley says "So the question is this, 'Can I sin a little bit here, and a little bit there and get by with it?' No you cannot."

2. However, throughout this video, he has stated you can live a life of unrepentant sin but you will still go to heaven.

3. This seems like you can sin, not repent, and get by with it.

CLASS QUESTION: How would you answer this?

AFTER DISCUSSION PLAY THE NEXT VIDEO SECTION.

Play Section 9 Response – 24:20- 28:11

CLASS QUESTION: Did you agree with their response?

CLASS QUESTION: Would you have made any other arguments?

- Have the class discuss the response.

TEACHERS NOTES FOR DISCUSSION IF NEEDED

1. Can a person sin and get away with it

without repenting?

2. Let's examine the Biblical example of Simon the Sorcerer in Acts 8

3. Acts 8:20 Simon the sorcerer was a Christian, sinned, told repent or perish

- perish apollumi "to destroy utterly"
- Thayer's Greek Lexicon "by ones conduct to cause another to lose eternal salvation"
- Same word John 10:28 "never perish"
  a. This statement in John 10:28 is conditional
  b. If you follow me, you will not perish, but if you don't follow me, you will perish.
  c. Simon was told if he did not follow God (by repenting of that sin in Acts 8:19-20) then he would perish with his money.
- This example leaves you with 2 options
  a. OSAS is true and The Apostle Peter was wrong. Therefore you can't trust your Bible or the apostles as inspired.
  b. OSAS is not true. Peter was right. Simon had to repent or perish eternally.

1. What other verses could be used against the positions a person is once saved, always saved?

- Galatians is written to those who

are already Christians, yet it warns those Christians that ... "Now the works of the flesh are evident, which are: adultery, fornication, uncleanness, lewdness, [20] idolatry, sorcery, hatred, contentions, jealousies, outbursts of wrath, selfish ambitions, dissensions, heresies, [21] envy, murders, drunkenness, revelries, and the like; of which I tell you beforehand, just as I also told you in time past, that those who practice such things will not inherit the kingdom of God." Galatians 5:19-21

- Galatians 6:7, same idea
- Romans 8:13 is written to Christians and in the context of Romans 8 which tells a Christian that they must live by the spirit and not by the flesh or they will die.
- "Brethren, if anyone among you wanders from the truth, and some-one turns him back, [20] let him know that he who turns a sinner from the error of his way will save a soul from death and cover a multitude of sins." James 5:19-20

While it is not true that a person who has salvation can never lose it, this should not cause a Christian to live in a constant state of fear

1. 1 John 5:13 says "These things I have written to you who believe in the name of the Son of God, that you may know

that you have eternal life, and that you may continue to believe in the name of the Son of God.

2. We can know we have eternal life based off God's Word and His Promises.

3. 1 John 1:4 states the purpose of this letter was so that our joy may be full

4. 1 John 1:6-10 uses the conditional statement word "if" 5 times to show that if we confess our sins to God, He is just and will cleanse us by the blood of His Son

5. Read John 1:6-10 if times permits and discuss among the class

6. 1 John 2:1-4 describes how Jesus is our attorney or advocate who will stand by our side and vouch for us before His Father so that we can have confidence on the day of Judgement (1 John 4:16-18).

7. For more study on knowing that we are saved and having confidence in salvation, watch Don Blackwell's Lessons on WVBS.org titled

- The Truth About Staying Saved
  a. https://video.wvbs.org/video/the-truth-about-staying-saved/

- Saved Without a Doubt
  a. https://video.wvbs.org/video/saved-without-a-doubt/

CLASS DISCUSSION: Did you agree/ like their arguments? Are there other passages you would have used?

FINAL SUMMARY DISCUSSION

CLASS QUESTIONS:

- Do you believe The Bible teaches a Christian can never do anything to be lost?

- Will God forgive any sin that we are willing to repent of?

- Does God have a limit to the times He will forgive us? No, Luke 17:3-4, Matthew 18:21-22

- What verses do you think are the strongest to show a Christian can sin, refuse to repent, and leave God and be lost?

If you or your students have any additional questions they would like answered, they are more than welcome to email Don and Aaron at **answeringtheerror@gbntv.org**

Tell the students that they can download the Gospel Broadcasting Network App to watch more episodes of Answering The Error and the many other programs that GBN has on their app and website www.GBNTV.org.

LESSON: **7**

EP. 3—WHY DO CATHOLICS BAPTIZE INFANTS?

Play Section 1 Intro/Arguments – 0:00-2:25

CLASS QUESTION: What argument/arguments did he make?

ARGUMENTS

1. He often gets the question "Why does the catholic church baptize babies/infants? Why not wait until they are old enough to make their own decision?"

2. He says that western culture is what makes us ask this question as we are used to making our own decisions in western culture. He then states we must look at how the church, Scripture and the history of the church (tradition) view that question as well.

CLASS QUESTION: How would you answer this?

AFTER DISCUSSION PLAY THE NEXT VIDEO SECTION.

Play Section 1 Response – 2:25-5:22

CLASS QUESTION: Did you agree with their response?

CLASS QUESTION: Would you have made any other arguments?

- Have the class discuss the response.

TEACHERS NOTES FOR DISCUSSION

1. Is this a cultural thing?

   - If we look at The Great Commission, we see that the Gospel and it's instructions were for all cultures and all people until the end of the world. Matthew 28:18-20, Mark 16:16

   - "All authority has been given to Me in heaven and on earth. [19] Go therefore and make disciples of **all the nations**, baptizing them in the name of the Father and of the Son and of the Holy Spirit, [20] teaching them to observe all things that I have commanded you; and lo, I am with you always, *even* to the end of the age." Mt. 28:18-20

   - "Go into all the world and preach the **gospel to every creature**. [16] He who believes and is baptized will be saved; but he who does not believe will be condemned." Mark 16:16

   - Also, faith is never inherited from others, but must be an individual choice for each person. Joshua 24:15 "choose for yourselves this day who you will serve"

2. Secondly, he stated we must look to Scripture, the church, and the history of the church (tradition)...

- Scripture

  a. We agree. 1 Peter 4:11 and Colossians 3:17 both teach that what we must speak as the oracles of God speak and have authority from Jesus Christ in everything that we do. We absolutely must have authority from Scripture to answer this question accurately.

- The church and it's history (Roman Catholic churches history)

  a. We disagree. Church history has been wrong many times over the course of the last 2000 years. In fact, just think about religious teachings today. We would probably agree a majority of modern churches teach many things wrong.

  b. Jude 3 says "the faith was once for all delivered to the saints"

    i. That means "once for all time"

  c. 2 Tim. 3:16-17 says "All Scripture *is* given by inspiration of God, and *is* profitable for doctrine, for reproof, for correction, for instruction in righteousness, [17] that the man of God may be complete, thoroughly equipped for every good work."

> i. We can be complete with Scripture alone without history.
>
> d. To be fair, we can look at history and if a doctrine never formerly taught springs out of thin air, we should be extra cautious, but ultimately Scripture is the only authority

CLASS DISCUSSION: Did you agree/ like their arguments? Are there other passages you would have used?

Play Section 2 Arguments – 5:22-5:29

CLASS QUESTION: What argument/arguments did he make?

ARGUMENTS

1. "We have to answer this question with both Scripture and tradition."

CLASS QUESTION: How would you answer this?

AFTER DISCUSSION PLAY THE NEXT VIDEO SECTION.

Play Section 2 Response – 5:29-7:09

CLASS QUESTION: Did you agree with their response?

CLASS QUESTION: Would you have made any other arguments?

- Have the class discuss the response.

TEACHERS NOTES FOR DISCUSSION

1. We agree as stated previously Scripture is what we use to answer this question.

2. We disagree that tradition is used to answer this question.

   - Now to clarify, there are different types of tradition. In many discussion with knowledgeable Catholics, they may bring us certain verse speaking to tradition and use them to support their arguments.

   - In Scripture, we must realize there are 2 types of traditions.

     a. Good Tradition to be followed that came from the Apostles spoken word and written word in Scripture.

        i. 2 Thessalonians 2:15

        ii. 2 Thessalonians 3:6

     b. Bad Traditions that are man-made, not inspired, and are not to be followed over the commands of God.

        i. Matthew 15:6-9, Mark 7:8

        ii. Colossians 2:8

CLASS DISCUSSION: Did you agree/ like their arguments? Are there other passages you would have used?

Play Section 3 Arguments – 7:09-7:28

CLASS QUESTION: What argument/arguments did he make?

ARGUMENTS

1. In the Old Testament, God brought young 8-day old babies into the covenant thru circumcision...

CLASS QUESTION: How would you answer this?

AFTER DISCUSSION PLAY THE NEXT VIDEO SECTION.

Play Section 3 Response – 7:28-9:23

CLASS QUESTION: Did you agree with their response?

CLASS QUESTION: Would you have made any other arguments?

- Have the class discuss the response.

TEACHERS NOTES FOR DISCUSSION

1. He is correct that in the Old Testament, the sign of the covenant given to Abraham was circumcision and this was a sign to be given to those children of God's people at 8 days old, only for the males.

2. However, the Old Testament Covenants are not equivalent to the New Covenant of Christianity. He is trying to make the argument since they included babies in the Covenant in the Old Testament, we should do the same thing in the New Testament

   - Does that mean that only males should be baptized? Females were

not circumcised so maybe we should not baptize females in the New Covenant.

3. Scripture even tells us there are differences between the Old Covenant circumcision given to Abraham and continued to the Jewish people in the Law of Moses.

- Jeremiah 31:34 speaking of a time when God would bring a new covenant in for His people which would replace the old covenant, Jeremiah wrote

    a. **Jer. 31:34** "No more shall every man teach his neighbor, and every man his brother, saying, 'Know the LORD,' for they all shall know Me, from the least of them to the greatest of them, says the LORD. For I will forgive their iniquity, and their sin I will remember no more."

    b. Notice the description of the Old Covenant is that people already in the covenant would have to be taught by their brethren. Why? Because they were born into the covenant physically at a young age and had not learned.

    c. Hebrews 8:11 quotes Jeremiah 31:34 and says the Old Covenant is obsolete and has been replaced by the new covenant.

- The New Covenant is different, peo-

ple are taught first and then baptized into the Covenant. They are born into this Covenant spiritually after being taught (John 6:44-45, John 3:3-5)

- The circumcision of the New Testament is not physical like the circumcision of the Old Testament, but it is a spiritual circumcision, made without hands. It is a circumcision where when one has faith in God and His Promises, they obey the command to be baptized and God cuts away their body of sins.

- Col. 2:11-12 "In Him you were also circumcised with the circumcision made without hands, by putting off the body of the sins of the flesh, by the circumcision of Christ, [12] buried with Him in baptism, in which you also were raised with *Him* through faith in the working of God, who raised Him from the dead."

  a. This passage shows that the one being baptized was raised with Christ "through faith in the working of God".

  b. An infant/baby does not have faith and thus could not have faith in the working of God when baptized.

  c. This itself rules out babies being candidates for baptism.

CLASS DISCUSSION: Did you agree/ like their arguments? Are there other passages you would have used?

Play Section 4 Arguments – 9:23-9:40

CLASS QUESTION: What argument/arguments did he make?

ARGUMENTS

1. He points to the idea that in the New Testament, there are many references to households being baptized, like Lydia and in Paul's writings.

CLASS QUESTION: How would you answer this?

AFTER DISCUSSION PLAY THE NEXT VIDEO SECTION.

Play Section 4 Response – 9:40-12:00

CLASS QUESTION: Did you agree with their response?

CLASS QUESTION: Would you have made any other arguments?

- Have the class discuss the response.

TEACHERS NOTES FOR DISCUSSION

1. The Bible does teach that households were baptized in the NT.

2. However, if you read each of these passages, you will notice that never does the Bible state that children were a part of these households.

3. If there were children in these households, would this not contradict the many other New Testament passages

77

that teach a person must meet other requirements before baptism?

- Mark 16:16 "he that believes and is baptized"

    a. Do babies believe in Jesus Christ before being baptized?

- Acts 2:38 "repent and be baptized"

    a. Do babies repent before being baptized?

- Acts 11:14 the household of Cornelius was told there would be "words by which he and his household would be saved"

    a. Do babies understand and comprehend a spoken message?

4. Here is a list of passages in the New Testament that refer to the baptism of households.

- Phil. 4:22 Paul says that the saints of Caesar's household greet the Philippian church. These are not babies or infants, but those who work for Caesar in his "household".

    b. According to prevailing usage, not members of the emperor's family or relationship, but servants at his court; in early imperial times they were ordinarily slaves or freedpersons (cp. Philo, In Flacc. 35; Jos., Ant. 17, 142; Arndt, William et al. *A Greek-English lexicon of the New Testament and other early Chris-*

tian literature 2000: 695. Print.

   i. Notice how this definition would exclude infants

   ii. It is possible that this definition could be used as we go through the other household passages. It also could be referring to actual blood relatives, but if so would only be speaking of those old enough to believe a message, comprehend it, response in repentance, before being baptized.

- Acts 16:15 household of Lydia

   a. Acts 16:14 says that Lydia was a seller of purple from Thyatira which was in western Asia Minor. She had traveled to Philippi which was in Greece. The traveled across the Mediterranean sea to sell purple. Do you think she had her newborn or infants with her on this journey?

- Acts 11:14 "words by which you and your household will be saved"

- Acts 16:31-34 "believe on Lord Jesus Christ, you and your household," "having believed in God with all his household"

- Acts 18:8 "Crispus believed on the Lord with all his household, and many of the Corinthians hearing, believed and were baptized."

a. Were there babies in these three households who comprehended the spoken message and believed? Or were there only adults in the household, who could believe? The latter makes more sense and does not contradict other Scriptures.

- 1 Cor. 1:16 "baptized the household of Stephanas"

a. Paul taught one must believe (Acts 16:30-34) and have faith in the working of God (Col. 2:11-12) prior to baptism. Would Paul have taught the household of Stephanas something different? No

CLASS DISCUSSION: Did you agree/ like their arguments? Are there other passages you would have used?

Play Section 5 Arguments – 12:01- 12:26

CLASS QUESTION: What argument/arguments did he make?

ARGUMENTS

1. He cites a few passages to support his point

2. First he cites "all that receive kingdom, receive gift of baptism" possibly thinking of John 3:3-5.

3. Then he references Matthew 19:14, Mark 10:14, Luke 18:16 by saying "He (Jesus) also refers to letting the little children come to him, not to hinder them"

4. He then connects these two passages together and uses them as support for the idea of baptizing infants.

CLASS QUESTION: How would you answer this?

AFTER DISCUSSION PLAY THE NEXT VIDEO SECTION.

Play Section 5 Response -12:26-15:06

CLASS QUESTION: Did you agree with their response?

CLASS QUESTION: Would you have made any other arguments?

- Have the class discuss the response.

TEACHERS NOTES FOR DISCUSSION

1. We need to pay very close attention sometimes when talking with others about ideas like this.

   - Notice how he jumped from one context to another.

   - He jumped from the context of John 3:3-5, which does speak of baptism, to the context of Matthew 19:13-14 which has nothing to do with baptism.

   - In Matthew 19:13, "people were bringing their children to Jesus so that Jesus could put his hands on them and pray for them."

   - In fact, in Matthew 19:14 Jesus then states "But Jesus said, "Let the little

81

children come to Me, and do not forbid them; for of such is the kingdom of
heaven."

a. Jesus compares the kingdom of
    heaven to little children. Jesus here
    supports the idea that children are
    innocent and do not even need to
    be baptized to have their sins for-
    given (Acts 2:38, Acts 22:16, 1 John
    3:4, Deut. 1:39).

b. Matthew 3:2 says that one must
    repent for the kingdom of heaven is
    at hand. Babies also cannot repent.
    There are many passages to show
    babies are not candidates for bap-
    tism. They have no need of it.

c. In Acts 8:35-38, the Ethiopian eu-
    nuch asked Philip, here is water,
    what hinders me from being bap-
    tized? And Phillip told the eunuch, if
    you believe with all your heart you
    many. Belief was a prerequisite here
    as well.

CLASS DISCUSSION: Did you agree/ like their arguments? Are there other passages you would have used?

LESSON: **8**

EP. 3—WHY DO CATHOLICS BAPTIZE INFANTS?

Play Section 6 Arguments – 15:06-15:24

CLASS QUESTION: What argument/arguments did he make?

ARGUMENTS

1. Here he points to church tradition and says "We know that the church has always done infant baptisms, we know this from the history of our church, even going back to earliest saints and church fathers, disciples of original apostles."

CLASS QUESTION: How would you answer this?

AFTER DISCUSSION PLAY THE NEXT VIDEO SECTION.

Play Section 6 Response – 15:24-16:42

CLASS QUESTION: Did you agree with their response?

CLASS QUESTION: Would you have made any other arguments?

- Have the class discuss the response.

TEACHERS NOTES FOR DISCUSSION

1. He argues that the entire history of the Christian church has supported infant baptism. This is not true. Here are a few early writers to take note of. While these men are not inspired, and Scripture is the only authority. We can see from their quotes, that infant baptism was not accepted in the early church.

   - The first possible mention of infant baptism may be from Irenaeus who lived from 140-203. He wrote in his work *Against Heresies 2.22.4* "*He (Christ) came to save, through the means of himself, all who through him are born again unto God, infants, children, boys, youths, and old men.*"

   - This however was not the accepted view. A contemporary of Irenaeus's named Tertullian wrote extensively on baptism and opposed the practice.

2. Tertullian who lived from (155-220) wrote a important document called "On Baptism". It shows us his stance on baptism during the early 3rd century (200-300AD), just 100 years after the apostles.

3. In chapter 18 he writes of baptism, "The

84

Lord does indeed say, Forbid them not to come unto me. Let them come, then, while they are growing up; let them come while they are learning, while they are learning whither to come; let them become <u>Christians</u> when they have become able to <u>know</u> Christ. Why does the innocent period of life hasten to the remission of <u>sins</u>? More caution will be exercised in worldly matters: so that one who is *not* trusted with earthly substance *is* trusted with divine! Let them <u>know</u> how to ask for <u>salvation</u>, that you may seem (at least) to have given to him that asks."

- Tertullian references Matthew 19:14 and says let them come to Jesus as they are growing up and learning and once they are able to know Christ, let them become Christians. He also thought belief was a prerequisite to baptism which would eliminate infant baptism.

- He also says that the innocent period of their lives (when they are children) does not need to rush (hasten) to the remission of sins. This shows that this early writer believed baptism was the point at which someone received the remission of sins. This can be seen throughout his writing "On Baptism".

- In fact, the very opening of his entire writing in chapter 1 says this. "Happy is our sacrament of water, in that, by

washing away the <u>sins</u> of our early blindness, we are set free *and admitted* into <u>eternal</u> life!"

4. Wayne Jackson's article "A History of the Baptism Apostasy" references multiple scholarly church historians, such as Augustus Neander and Philip Schaff, who although they themselves are strong proponents of infant baptism, admit that the practice of the early church was not to baptize infants but only to adults as faith and baptism were connected. Here is an excerpt from that article.

- "Even Philip Schaff, a member of the Reformed Church, and a strong pedo-baptist advocate, was forced to admit that "adult baptism was the rule, infant baptism the exception" until the church was fairly established in the Roman Empire. He points out that Augustine, Gregory Nazianzen, and Chrysostom had "Christian" mothers, yet these men were not baptized until early manhood (210).

- The article and citations can be found here.

   a. https://christiancourier.com/articles/a-history-of-the-baptism-apostasy

Even with these facts, we must once again state that church tradition has been consistently wrong throughout history when not based directly on Scripture. We must always seek

to back up what we teach with Scripture (1 Peter 4:11, 2 Tim. 3:16-17, Col. 3:17).

CLASS DISCUSSION: Did you agree/ like their arguments? Are there other passages you would have used?

Play Section 7 Arguments – 16:42- 17:27

CLASS QUESTION: What argument/arguments did he make?

ARGUMENTS

1. He mentions the names of Irenaus, Hippolytus, and Augustine and even the church council of Carthage

CLASS QUESTION: How would you answer this?

AFTER DISCUSSION PLAY THE NEXT VIDEO SECTION.

Play Section 7 Response – 17:27- 19:04

CLASS QUESTION: Did you agree with their response?

CLASS QUESTION: Would you have made any other arguments?

- Have the class discuss the response.

TEACHERS NOTES FOR DISCUSSION

1. Irenaeus who we mentioned earlier may have been the first to reference it. The other examples he references are much later. Augustine lived in the late 4th cen-

tury and the Council of Carthage was in 411 AD. These examples are hundreds of years after the apostles. Also this doctrine is not taught by all his contemporaries, but it seems all the contemporary's taught baptism for the remission of sins, after one believed and repented.

- More information and citations can be found here.

  a. https://christiancourier.com/articles/a-history-of-the-baptism-apostasy

  b. What Early Christians Believed About Baptism – Bible.ca

- This shows that the early church after the apostles taught baptism for the remission of sins for those who could believe and repent.

- The man-made tradition of infant baptism did not come until after the apostles.

- 2 Timothy 3:16-17 shows that All Scripture is given by inspiration of God, and is profitable for doctrine, for reproof, for correction, for instruction in righteousness, that the man of God may be complete, thoroughly equipped for every good work.

  a. Notice this verse says that Scripture thoroughly equips us, and we can be complete with it. We do not need tradition to prove a Bible teaching.

b. The only traditions we need to follow are inspired traditions from the apostles.

c. 2 Thess. 2:15 "Therefore, brethren, stand fast and hold the traditions which you were taught, whether by word or our epistle."

d. 2 Thess. 3:6 "But we command you, brethren, in the name of our Lord Jesus Christ, that you withdraw from every brother who walks disorderly and not according to the tradition which he received from us."

CLASS DISCUSSION: Did you agree/ like their arguments? Are there other passages you would have used?

Play Section 8 Arguments – 19:04- 19:45

CLASS QUESTION: What argument/arguments did he make?

ARGUMENTS

1. "Baptism is the point at which original sin is washed away and thus we should want to give that gift to everyone"

CLASS QUESTION: How would you answer this?

AFTER DISCUSSION PLAY THE NEXT VIDEO SECTION.

Play Section 8 Response -19:45-23:54

CLASS QUESTION: Did you agree with their response?

CLASS QUESTION: Would you have made any other arguments?

- Have the class discuss the response.

TEACHERS NOTES FOR DISCUSSION

1. What is original sin? This is the idea that some groups teach that everyone inherits the sin of Adam when they are born and thus they need to be baptized to have that original sin washed away. This is one of the main reasons the Roman Catholic church baptizes babies.

2. The Bible however does not teach the doctrine of original sin.

3. The entire chapter of Ezekiel 18 speaks about a proverb that was in Israel that was similar to the idea that a son is guilty of a fathers behavior (Ezekiel 18:2). Ezekiel teaches this is not how God operates and Ezekiel 18:20 is one of the clearest passages to refute the idea we inherit the sin of Adam.

   - Ezekiel 18:20 "The soul who sins shall die. The son shall not bear the guilt of the father, nor the father bear the guilt of the son. The righteousness of the righteous shall be upon himself, and the wickedness of the wicked shall be upon himself."

4. It teaches that babies are born innocent

not knowing good or evil (Deut. 1:39, Jer. 19:4-6).

5. The Bible teaches that the qualities of little children are models for us to emulate, not that they are corrupt sinners.

6. Matthew 18:2-4 "Then Jesus called a little child to Him, set him in the midst of them, and said, "Assuredly, I say to you, unless you are converted and become as little children, you will by no means enter the kingdom of heaven. Therefore whoever humbles himself as this little child is the greatest in the kingdom of heaven."

7. Matthew 19:14"But Jesus said, "Let the little children come to Me, and do not forbid them; for of such is the kingdom of heaven."

8. Paul himself said in Romans 7:9 that he "was alive once without the law, but when the commandment came, sin revived and I died."

- Paul here is pointing to the fact that at some point in his life he was spiritually alive. Then the commandment came, sin revived, and he died spiritually. This is referring to the idea that Paul, who was born under the law of Moses, was spiritually not accountable to the law when he was younger. As he grew in understanding he eventually realized what the law said and when he broke it he died spiritually.

This shows Paul was not born guilty of Adam's Sin

9. Another implication of this doctrine is that if babies are born inheriting the sin of Adam, what happens to babies that die? Would they be lost?

- If yes, that does not seem like God to punish one for the sins of another. Scripture teaches against this (Ezekiel 18).

- If no, how can they be saved while having sin?

- David's small child died at 7 days old in 2 Samuel and he said...

   a. 2 Samuel 12:23- "Who can tell *whether* the Lord will be gracious to me, that the child may live?' [23] But now he is dead; why should I fast? Can I bring him back again? I shall go to him, but he shall not return to me."

10. Two questions that you can ask to people who believe this are

- If we have a sinful nature from original sin, that causes us to sin, why did Adam and Eve sin?

   a. Adam and Eve did not inherit any sin. They were pure and innocent. Yet they had free will and they chose to sin.

- If we have a sinful nature from original sin, that causes us to sin, did Jesus have a sinful nature?

a. Hebrews 4:15 and Hebrews 2:17 say that Jesus was tempted in all points like were are and Jesus was made like us in all things (in regards to temptation). How can we have a sin nature that causes us to sin and Jesus not have one, and Heb. 2:17 and Heb. 4:15 be accurate?

   i. Heb. 2:17 "Therefore, in all things He had to be made like His brethren, that He might be a merciful and faithful High Priest in things pertaining to God, to make propitiation for the sins of the people."

   ii. Heb. 4:15 "For we do not have a High Priest who cannot sympathize with our weaknesses, but was in all points tempted as we are, yet without sin."

CLASS DISCUSSION: Did you agree/ like their arguments? Are there other passages you would have used?

Play Section 9 Arguments – 23:54-24:55

CLASS QUESTION: What argument/arguments did he make?

ARGUMENTS

1. "We want to give our children the best gifts, therefore we should want to baptize our children."

CLASS QUESTION: How would you answer this?

AFTER DISCUSSION PLAY THE NEXT VIDEO SECTION.

Play Section 9 Response -24:55-25:15

CLASS QUESTION: Did you agree with their response?

CLASS QUESTION: Would you have made any other arguments?

- Have the class discuss the response.

TEACHERS NOTES FOR DISCUSSION

1. We do want to give our children the best gifts! We love our children.

2. The best gift as Christian parents we can give our children, is to teach them about God and teach them His Word. The best thing we can do is to teach them what the Bible teaches. Teach them to rely on God's Word alone.

3. We should teach them the principles of 1 Peter 4:11, 2 Tim. 3:16-17, and Col. 3:17 that Scripture is the authority, and we need to have God's authority for the things we do and teach. Teach them to study 2 Tim. 2:15.

CLASS DISCUSSION: Did you agree/ like their arguments? Are there other passages you would have used?

Play Section 10 Arguments – 25:15-26:11

CLASS QUESTION: What argument/arguments did he make?

ARGUMENTS

1. He makes the statement that the best way to raise a child spiritually is to make that promise that you will raise that child to know Christ and His words, His love, and His teaching.

Class Question: How would you answer this?

AFTER DISCUSSION PLAY THE NEXT VIDEO SECTION.

Play Section 10 Response – 26:11 – 27:24

CLASS QUESTION: Did you agree with their response?

CLASS QUESTION: Would you have made any other arguments?

- Have the class discuss the response.

TEACHERS NOTES FOR DISCUSSION

1. We should seek to raise our children in the best possible spiritual manner. We agree on that. The place where we disagree is the method. He states that this infant baptism practice is to make a promise that you will raise that child to know Christ and His Words, teaching, and love.

2. How can we teach a child to love Jesus's teaching by teaching them something

that Jesus didn't teach?

3. Jesus taught a pre-requisite to baptism was belief which a child cannot do (Mark 16:16).

4. Paul wrote to Timothy "that from childhood you have known the Holy Scriptures, which are able to make you wise for salvation through faith which is in Christ Jesus." 2 Tim. 3:15

   - Paul wrote to Timothy that the Scriptures were able to make him wise for salvation. How? Through faith which in Jesus Christ. An infant is not capable of knowledge and faith.

5. We should teach our children Scripture and let Scripture be their guide

   - 2 Tim. 2:15 "Be diligent to present yourself approved to God, a worker who does not need to be ashamed, rightly dividing the word of truth."

   - 2 Tim. 3:14-17 "But you must continue in the things which you have learned and been assured of, knowing from whom you have learned them, and that from childhood you have known the Holy Scriptures, which are able to make you wise for salvation through faith which is in Christ Jesus. All Scripture is given by inspiration of God, and is profitable for doctrine, for reproof, for correction, for instruction in righteousness, that the man of God may be complete, thoroughly equipped for every good work."

CLASS DISCUSSION: Did you agree/ like their arguments? Are there other passages you would have used?

FINAL SUMMARY DISCUSSION

CLASS QUESTIONS:

- Do you believe The Bible teaches that baptism is for babies or those who are old enough to have faith?

- What are some verses you remember that show baptism is not something babies can do? Mark 16:16, Acts 2:38

- Do babies inherit the sin of Adam, sometimes called Original Sin? No Ezekiel 18:20

- What verses do you think are the strongest to show a babies are sinless? Ezekiel 18:20, Jer. 19:4-6, 1 John 3:4, Deut. 1:39, Romans 7:9

If you or your students have any additional questions they would like answered, they are more than welcome to email Don and Aaron at **answeringtheerror@gbntv.org**

Tell the students that they can download the Gospel Broadcasting Network App to watch more episodes of Answering The Error and the many other programs that GBN has on their app and website www.GBNTV.org.

LESSON: **9**

EP. 4—WHY DO I HAVE TO CONFESS MY SINS TO A PRIEST?

Play Section 1 Intro/Arguments – 0:00-1:58

CLASS QUESTION: What argument/arguments did he make?

ARGUMENTS

1. He asks the question "Father, why do we have to confess our sins to a priest and why can't we just confess our sins directly to God?"

CLASS QUESTION: How would you answer this?

AFTER DISCUSSION PLAY THE NEXT VIDEO SECTION.

Play Section 1 Response – 1:58- 4:52

CLASS QUESTION: Did you agree with their response?

Class Question: Would you have made any other arguments?

- Have the class discuss the response.

TEACHERS NOTES FOR DISCUSSION

1. He addresses himself or other Catholic priests as "Father".

2. In Matthew 23:9, Jesus spoke against the idea of using religious titles to set one person above another. He said "Do not call anyone on earth your father; for One is your Father, He who is in heaven."

   - This is not saying it is wrong to refer to your earthly father as father in a hereditary sense as we see many Biblical examples of this

   - Luke 15:21 "And the son said to him, 'Father, I have sinned against heaven and in your sight, and am no longer worthy to be called your son."

   - John 8:56, "Your father Abraham rejoiced to see my day."

   - Ezekiel 18:20, "The soul that sinneth, it shall die. The son shall not bear the iniquity of the father"

3. What about passages like 1 Cor. 4:15 "I became your father through the gospel" or 1 Peter 5:13 "my son Mark"?

4. Notice that these are not a special religious title, but describing a relationship. This is just like 2 Peter 3:15, where Peter called Paul "his beloved brother." This was referring to a spiritual relationship, not a religious title.

5. Why can't we go to God directly? Valid Question Peter should be a good one to look to. Acts 2:37-38, Acts 8:20-22

CLASS DISCUSSION: Did you agree/ like their arguments? Are there other passages you would have used?

Play Section 2 Arguments – 4:52-5:21

CLASS QUESTION: What argument/arguments did he make?

ARGUMENTS

1. He says that to answer this question, "we have to look back to the history and the tradition of the church."

Class Question: How would you answer this?

AFTER DISCUSSION PLAY THE NEXT VIDEO SECTION.

Play Section 2 Response – 5:21-7:10

CLASS QUESTION: Did you agree with their response?

CLASS QUESTION: Would you have made any other arguments?

- Have the class discuss the response.

TEACHERS NOTES FOR DISCUSSION

1. Scripture should be our authority for all we do in Christianity

> • 2 Tim. 2:15, 3:16-17, Col. 3:17
>
> 2. When one does not have Scripture to back their position they will appeal to tradition or church history. They are not referring to church tradition as in the words or deeds of the apostles (2 Thess. 2:15, 3:6), but rather to man-made tradition from uninspired men (Matthew 15:6-9, Col. 2:18).

CLASS DISCUSSION: Did you agree/ like their arguments? Are there other passages you would have used?

Play Section 3 Arguments – 7:10-8:13

CLASS QUESTION: What argument/arguments did he make?

ARGUMENTS

1.   He refers to the story in Mark 2 where the paralytic was lowered through the roof and Jesus told the man in Mark 2:5-12 that his sins were forgiven

CLASS QUESTION: How would you answer this?

AFTER DISCUSSION PLAY THE NEXT VIDEO SECTION.

Play Section 3 Response – 8:13-11:26

CLASS QUESTION: Did you agree with their response?

CLASS QUESTION: Would you have made any other arguments?

- Have the class discuss the response.

TEACHERS NOTES FOR DISCUSSION

1. To make his point that we should confess our sins to a priest, he tells the account of the paralyzed man in <u>Mark 2</u>. He's the one who was lowered down through the roof. And in Mark 2:5, Jesus tells the man, "Son, your sins are forgiven you."

2. Well, some of the scribes are shocked and say that Jesus is speaking blasphemy.... and here's their reasoning, "Why can forgive sins but God alone?"

3. Jesus doesn't dispute their point...He does a miracle to prove that He is God and therefore has the power to forgive sins.

4. Mark 2:10, "But that you may know that the Son of Man has power on earth to forgive sins"—He said to the paralytic, [11] "I say to you, arise, take up your bed, and go to your house." [12] Immediately he arose, took up the bed, and went out in the presence of them all, so that all were amazed and glorified God, saying, "We never saw *anything* like this!"

   a. Now, sometimes men will focus particularly on Matthew's account of this in Matthew 9:2-8. Verse 8 says that, "Now when the multitudes saw *it*, they marveled and glorified God, who had given such power to men."

   b. This passage is not teaching that God gave power to men to forgive

sins, but rather they glorified God that God had given such power to mankind referring to that power displayed in Jesus Christ who was a man in their eyes.

c. **KEY POINT**: Notice that the key point of this entire story is that only God can forgive sins, not mere men.

5. Later in the Gospels, when Jesus gives the Great Commission, notice that the apostles were to preach the conditions of forgiveness such as belief in the Gospel, belief and baptism (Mark 16:15-16). They were not able to forgive sins themselves, but preach the conditions and when people obeyed those conditions, they were forgiven by God.

CLASS DISCUSSION: Did you agree/ like their arguments? Are there other passages you would have used?

Play Section 4 Arguments – 11:26-11:48

CLASS QUESTION: What argument/arguments did he make?

ARGUMENTS

1. Now, he strings together several passages.

2. He begins with John 20:21, "With the same authority that I have been sent, I now send you."

CLASS QUESTION: How would you answer this?

AFTER DISCUSSION PLAY THE NEXT VIDEO SECTION.

Play Section 4 Response – 11:48-15:26

CLASS QUESTION: Did you agree with their response?

CLASS QUESTION: Would you have made any other arguments?

- Have the class discuss the response.

TEACHERS NOTES FOR DISCUSSION

1. He doesn't mention this, but the Catholic church particularly focuses on verse 23 of this chapter, where Jesus said, "If you forgive the sins of any, they are forgiven them; if you retain the sins of any, they are retained."

   - He is trying to make the argument Jesus could forgive sins and then he gave that authority to forgive sins to the apostles in John 20:23.

   - In John 20:22 Jesus breathed on the apostles and said "receive the Holy Spirit."

   - This is a confusing text to some, but Jesus is prophetically telling them they will receive the Holy Spirit and will preach the terms by which sins will be forgiven. This is not Jesus giving them personal authority to personally forgive sins as they see fit.

   - HOW DO WE KNOW THIS?

a. In all other 3 Gospel accounts of Matthew, Mark, and Luke, the Great Commission is given to the apostles to teach certain things which will lead to salvation and forgiveness of sins.

b. We will focus in on Mark and Luke's accounts specifically and note things from those two accounts.

c. Matthew 28:18-20 "And Jesus came and spoke to them, saying, "All authority has been given to Me in heaven and on earth. Go therefore and make disciples of all the nations, baptizing them in the name of the Father and of the Son and of the Holy Spirit, teaching them to observe all things that I have commanded you; and lo, I am with you always, even to the end of the age." Amen.

d. Mark 16:15-16 "And He said to them, "Go into all the world and preach the gospel to every creature. He who believes and is baptized will be saved; but he who does not believe will be condemned."

    i. Notice the apostles were to preach the Gospel and the terms of forgiveness to which God would forgive the sins, not to forgive sins themselves.

e. Luke 24:46-49 "Then He said to

them, 'Thus it is written, and thus it was necessary for the Christ to suffer and to rise from the dead the third day, and that repentance and remission of sins should be preached in His name to all nations, beginning at Jerusalem. And you are witnesses of these things. "Behold, I send the Promise of My Father upon you; but tarry in the city of Jerusalem until you are endued with power from on high.'"

i. Notice here that Jesus said that repentance and remission of sins would not begin until Jerusalem, which was the Day of Pentecost in Acts 2.

ii. Notice also in Luke 24:49 Jesus said they were to wait in Jerusalem until they were endued with power from on high. That power was the baptism of the Holy Spirit they were to receive on the day of Pentecost as Acts 2 records.

iii. In Acts 1:4,5,8 they were still waiting for that promise.

- "And being assembled together with them, He commanded them not to depart from Jerusalem, but to wait for the Promise of the Father, "which," He said, "you have heard from Me; for John truly

baptized with water, but you shall be baptized with the Holy Spirit not many days from now…But you shall receive power when the Holy Spirit has come upon you; and you shall be witnesses to Me in Jerusalem, and in all Judea and Samaria, and to the end of the earth." Acts 1:4,5,8

iv. If John 20:22 was an actual account of them receiving the Holy Spirit, then there would be a contradiction between the accounts of John and Luke/Acts.

2. And then he references Matthew 16:19 where Jesus told Peter "whatever you bind on earth will be bound in heaven, and whatever you loose on earth will be loosed in heaven."

- These are future perfect passives in Greek which are more accurately translated in the New American Standard Bible translation. Look how they translated this passage.

- Mt. 16:18-19 "I will give you the keys of the kingdom of heaven; and whatever you bind on earth shall have been bound in heaven, and whatever you loose on earth shall have been loosed in heaven."

- Just like John 20:20-23, this passage was a promise to the apostles that when they were inspired by the Holy Spirit, they would not be able to forgive sins personally, but they would preach the terms of forgiveness from God.

- Thus, what God had already determined and bound in heaven (the terms of forgiveness) they will bind on earth through the authority of teaching as apostles.

3. If there was still any confusion at all, we can look to Acts 2 on the day of Pentecost when Peter preached the Gospel to those Jews gathered there for the first time. Those people asked what to do to have their sins forgiven and Peter responded in Acts 2:38 not with "I forgive your sins", but rather Peter preached God's message of forgiveness.

- Acts 2:38 "Then Peter said to them, "Repent, and let every one of you be baptized in the name of Jesus Christ for the remission of sins; and you shall receive the gift of the Holy Spirit."

CLASS DISCUSSION: Did you agree/ like their arguments? Are there other passages you would have used?

LESSON: **10**

EP. 4—WHY DO I HAVE TO CONFESS MY SINS TO A PRIEST?

Play Section 5 Arguments – 15:26-15:45

CLASS QUESTION: What argument/arguments did he make?

ARGUMENTS

1. He says that "again and again we have these scriptural backings...where Jesus tells them to go forth, to baptize and to forgive sins..."

2. He says, "again and again" he's provided scripture to support priests forgiving sins.

3. Then he says that Jesus sent "the priests, the apostles, the bishops to do those same things" ...that is to baptize and to forgive sins.

CLASS QUESTION: How would you answer this?

AFTER DISCUSSION PLAY THE NEXT VIDEO SECTION.

Play Section 5 Response – 15:45-19:51

CLASS QUESTION: Did you agree with their response?

CLASS QUESTION: Would you have made any other arguments?

- Have the class discuss the response.

TEACHERS NOTES FOR DISCUSSION

1. He says that "again and again we have these scriptural backings...where Jesus tells them to go forth, to baptize and to forgive sins..." He says, "again and again" he's provided scripture to support priests forgiving sins.

   - He has provided Scriptures, but we have examined these to see how he has taken those passages out of context and misapplied them. He has strung passages together from different contexts together to make it seem like he has Scriptural support for this idea.

2. Then he says that Jesus sent "the priests, the apostles, the bishops to do those same things" ...that is to baptize and to forgive sins.

   - The Bible does not teach this.

   - This idea stems from the idea that some groups like the Catholic church have different roles in that they call some clergy and other are laity. How-

ever in the New Testament, all Christians are called priests and saints.

- 1 Peter 2:9 - "But you *are* a chosen generation, a royal priesthood, a holy nation"

3. Secondly, he says that Jesus told the "bishops" to do these things.

- A bishop in the New Testament is a leader of a local church congregation. He must be qualified according to what 1 Timothy 3 and Titus 1 describe.

- 1 Tim. 3:1, "This *is* a faithful saying: If a man desires the position of a bishop, he desires a good work. [2] A bishop then must be blameless, the husband of one wife, temperate, sober-minded, of good behavior, hospitable, able to teach..."

- The word "bishop" in this passage is just another word for elder. The Greek word here for "bishop" is EPISKAPAE.

   a. This is from Thayer's Greek Lexicon. "Among the Christians, those who presided over the assemblies or churches; the NT uses the words Bishops, Elders, and Presbyters interchangeably."

   b. The word shepherd, or pastor in Eph. 4:11, also refers to this office of an elder. In Acts 20:17, Paul called for the elders of the church. Acts 20:28 says the Holy Spirit made

> them overseers to shepherd (pastor) the flock.
>
> - This idea that a bishop is a special title in a religious hierarchy as in the Roman Catholic church is not accurate.

CLASS DISCUSSION: Did you agree/ like their arguments? Are there other passages you would have used?

Play Section 6 Arguments – 19:51- 20:00

CLASS QUESTION: What argument/arguments did he make?

ARGUMENTS

1. "When we go to confession, it's not easy, why do I have to go in and confess these sins to a priest?"

CLASS QUESTION: How would you answer this?

AFTER DISCUSSION PLAY THE NEXT VIDEO SECTION.

Play Section 6 Response -20:00-22:30

CLASS QUESTION: Did you agree with their response?

CLASS QUESTION: Would you have made any other arguments?

- Have the class discuss the response.

TEACHERS NOTES FOR DISCUSSION

1. He speaks as if he's already established that we have to go to confession.

2. I would make this argument, if we do have to go to confession, as he says it, shouldn't there be an example of this somewhere in the Bible?

3. We don't see any example of this in the Bible.

   - We already discussed how Peter in Acts 2:38 gave the terms of forgiveness to become a Christian.

   - What about an example of some-one who was already a Christian and needed sins forgiven?

     a. Later in the book of Acts, Peter gives another example of how to have sins forgiven and this is after Simon the Sorcerer has become a Chris-tian. Simon sinned and Peter did not forgive his sins directly, but Peter told him to repent and pray to God.

        i. Acts 8:20-22 "But Peter said to him, "Your money perish with you, because you thought that the gift of God could be purchased with money! You have neither part nor portion in this matter, for your heart is not right in the sight of God. Repent therefore of this your wickedness, and pray God if perhaps the thought of your heart may be forgiven you."

CLASS DISCUSSION: Did you agree/ like their arguments? Are there other passages you would have used?

Play Section 7 Arguments – 22:30-22:41

CLASS QUESTION: What argument/arguments did he make?

ARGUMENTS

1. "He says, when we go to God, we ask for forgiveness."

CLASS QUESTION: How would you answer this? Is this correct?

AFTER DISCUSSION PLAY THE NEXT VIDEO SECTION.

Play Section 7 Response – 22:41-23:23

CLASS QUESTION: Did you agree with their response?

CLASS QUESTION: Would you have made any other arguments?

- Have the class discuss the response.

TEACHERS NOTES FOR DISCUSSION

1. That's correct. He is correct in stating that when we do something wrong we go to God for forgiveness

   - In Luke 14:2-4 – where Jesus was teaching how to pray, he said, "Our Father in heaven, ... forgive us our sins,

For we also forgive everyone who is indebted to us."

- It's interesting that we pray the Father for forgiveness of our sins. We don't go through a priest to do this.

CLASS DISCUSSION: Did you agree/ like their arguments? Are there other passages you would have used?

Play Section 8 Arguments – 23:23-23:57

CLASS QUESTION: What argument/arguments did he make?

ARGUMENTS

1. "When we sin against someone privately we need to go to them to be reconciled with them and reconcile ourselves with God."

CLASS QUESTION: How would you answer this? Is this correct?

AFTER DISCUSSION PLAY THE NEXT VIDEO SECTION.

Play Section 8 Response – 23:57- 24:36

CLASS QUESTION: Did you agree with their response?

CLASS QUESTION: Would you have made any other arguments?

- Have the class discuss the response.

TEACHERS NOTES FOR DISCUSSION

1. We agree with him here. If we sin against someone privately, the Bible has given us a process in Matthew 18:15-20.

2. Matthew 18:15-20 "Moreover if your brother sins against you, go and tell him his fault between you and him alone. If he hears you, you have gained your brother. But if he will not hear, take with you one or two more, that 'by the mouth of two or three witnesses every word may be established.' And if he refuses to hear them, tell it to the church. But if he refuses even to hear the church, let him be to you like a heathen and a tax collector. "Assuredly, I say to you, whatever you bind on earth will be bound in heaven, and whatever you loose on earth will be loosed in heaven. "Again I say to you that if two of you agree on earth concerning anything that they ask, it will be done for them by My Father in heaven. For where two or three are gathered together in My name, I am there in the midst of them."

3. Mt. 5:23 "Therefore if you bring your gift to the altar, and there remember that your brother has something against you, leave your gift there before the altar, and go your way. First be reconciled to your brother, and then come and offer your gift."

CLASS DISCUSSION: Did you agree/ like their arguments? Are there other passages you would have used?

Play Section 9 Arguments – 24:36-24:46

CLASS QUESTION: What argument/arguments did he make?

ARGUMENTS

1. He says that when we go to confession, the priest is sitting in the Persona Christi, and Christ is working through the priest to forgive us.

CLASS QUESTION: How would you answer this?

AFTER DISCUSSION PLAY THE NEXT VIDEO SECTION.

Play Section 9 Response – 24:46-28:05

CLASS QUESTION: Did you agree with their response?

CLASS QUESTION: Would you have made any other arguments?

- Have the class discuss the response.

TEACHERS NOTES FOR DISCUSSION

1. First, nowhere in the Bible do we find this phrase "persona Christi" or this idea of Christ working through a priest to forgive our sins.

   - Persona Christi is "a Latin phrase meaning "in the person of Christ" and this is an important concept in Roman Catholicism. They state that the priest is in **persona Christi**, because he acts

as Christ and as God.

- The Catholic Catechism – "possesses the authority to act in the power and place of the person of Christ himself."

- There is no Biblical evidence to support this.

2. Scripture teaches there is One Mediator between God and men, and that mediator is Jesus, not a Roman Catholic priest

- 1 Tim. 2:5 "For *there is* one God and one Mediator between God and men, *the* Man Christ Jesus"

3. If this is true, why don't we see this one time in Scripture?

- In Scripture sins are forgiven by God when one becomes a Christian initially, through belief, repentance, confession and baptism to have sins washed away (John 8:24, Rom. 10:9–10, Acts 2:38, 22:16). Once that person is a Christian, when he sins, he repents and confesses his sins to God (Acts 8:20–22, 1 John 1:6–9).

CLASS DISCUSSION: Did you agree/ like their arguments? Are there other passages you would have used?

FINAL CLASS DISCUSSION

Questions:

- Do you believe The Bible teaches a person must

confess their sins to another person for God to forgive them?

Acts 8:20-22, 1 John 1:6-9, Matthew 6:12

- Did the apostles have the authority to forgive sins themselves? Or were they only preaching God's terms of forgiveness?

  Mark 2:10, Mark 16:15-16, Luke 24:47, Acts 2:37-38

- Are only special Christians priests or are all Christians priests?

  1 Peter 2:5,9

If you or your students have any additional questions they would like answered, they are more than welcome to email Don and Aaron at **answeringtheerror@gbntv.org**

Tell the students that they can download the Gospel Broadcasting Network App to watch more episodes of Answering The Error and the many other programs that GBN has on their app and website www.GBNTV.org.

LESSON: **11**

EP. 5—THE SINNERS PRAYER?

Play Section 1 Intro/Arguments – 0:00-2:13

CLASS QUESTION: What argument/arguments did he make?

ARGUMENTS

1. Mr. Hagee says that the greatest question in the Bible is "What will you do with Jesus? How do you come to the saving knowledge of Jesus Christ?"

CLASS QUESTION: How would you answer this? Do you agree?

AFTER DISCUSSION PLAY THE NEXT VIDEO SECTION.

Play Section 1 Response – 2:13-2:53

CLASS QUESTION: Did you agree with their response?

CLASS QUESTION: Would you have made any other arguments?

- Have the class discuss the response.

TEACHERS NOTES FOR DISCUSSION

1. We do agree with this statement! Mr. Hagee is correct. "What will you do with Jesus? How do you come to the saving knowledge of Jesus Christ?" are the most important questions a person can ask themselves.

2. John 12:48 says "He who rejects Me, and does not receive My words, has that which judges him—the word that I have spoken will judge him in the last day."

3. This question "What must I do to be saved?" is asked a few times in the Bible. Some examples are Acts 2:37, 16:30, 9:6,22:10?

CLASS DISCUSSION: Did you agree/ like their arguments? Are there other passages you would have used?

| Play Section 2 Arguments – 2:53-3:30 |

CLASS QUESTION: What argument/arguments did he make?

ARGUMENTS

1. Next he states "First, you recognize that you need Christ...that you have sinned and come short of the glory of God"(Romans 3:23). He points out that our goodness cannot save us,

helping the poor cannot save us, but only the blood of Christ can save us."

CLASS QUESTION: How would you answer this? Do you agree with this?

AFTER DISCUSSION PLAY THE NEXT VIDEO SECTION.

Play Section 2 Response – 3:30-4:12

CLASS QUESTION: Did you agree with their response?

CLASS QUESTION: Would you have made any other arguments?

- Have the class discuss the response.

TEACHERS NOTES FOR DISCUSSION

1. Absolutely we agree with all of this.
2. Romans 3:23 tells us that we all have sinned and fall short of God's glory. Sin is what separates us from God (Is. 59:1-2). Hence, we need to be reconciled to God, justified before Him, and have our sins forgiven. The Bible teaches that the blood of Christ does all of these things (Rev. 1:5, Col. 1:20, Rom. 5:9). The blood of Christ also redeems us (Eph. 1:7, Col. 1:14).

CLASS DISCUSSION: Did you agree/ like their arguments? Are there other passages you would have used?

Play Section 3 Arguments – 4:12- 4:25

CLASS QUESTION: What argument/arguments did he make?

ARGUMENTS

1. He quotes I John 1:9, "If we confess our sins, He is faithful and just to forgive us *our* sins and to cleanse us from all unrighteousness."

   - HINT: He is proceeding to use this verse as the way sins are forgiven for non-Christians to become Christians.

CLASS QUESTION: How would you answer this?

AFTER DISCUSSION PLAY THE NEXT VIDEO SECTION.

Play Section 3 Response – 4:25-6:30

CLASS QUESTION: Did you agree with their response?

CLASS QUESTION: Would you have made any other arguments?

- Have the class discuss the response.

TEACHERS NOTES FOR DISCUSSION

1. This is a beautiful verse, however he is going to take this passage out of context. 1 John 1 is written to those who are already Christians (1 John 2:7).

2. The Bible teaches that there is a process a person has their sins forgiven initially to become a Christian. Once

that happens, their sins are remitted by repentance, confession and prayer (Acts 8:20-22, 1 John 1:7-9).

3. We are discussing a person who is a non-Christian in this video and what they need to do to be forgiven of their sins. Never in the New Testament under the Christian dispensation that started in Acts 2 is someone told to confess their sins to be forgiven, unless it is in conjunction with belief (John 8:24), repentance (Acts 17:30) and baptism in water (Acts 2:38, 22:16).

4. In Acts 8:12-22, we can see the story of Simon the Sorcerer. He is taught, believes, and is baptized. His sins are forgiven, and he begins to follow Philip who taught him. He then sins and is not told to be re-baptized, but simply to repent and pray to God for forgiveness. This is a parallel situation to 1 John 1:7-9 which Mr. Hagee has quoted.

CLASS DISCUSSION: Did you agree/ like their arguments? Are there other passages you would have used?

Play Section 4 Arguments – 6:30-7:04

CLASS QUESTION: What argument/arguments did he make?

ARGUMENTS

1. He says "God can save to the uttermost. It makes

no difference what you have done. His amazing grace can reach you. He loves us even though we have rebelled against Him. He quotes Romans 5:8-9 and says God made it possible through the gift of his Son, for you, and for me to be saved."

CLASS QUESTION: How would you answer this?

AFTER DISCUSSION PLAY THE NEXT VIDEO SECTION.

Play Section 4 Response – 7:04-8:14

CLASS QUESTION: Did you agree with their response?

CLASS QUESTION: Would you have made any other arguments?

- Have the class discuss the response.

TEACHERS NOTES FOR DISCUSSION

1. We agree 100% with everything he stated in this segment.
   - God can save to the uttermost (Heb. 7:25, Luke 19:10).
   - God's love and grace has been delivered to us and brought salvation (John 3:16, Titus 2:11-12).
   - "But God demonstrates His own love toward us, in that while we were still sinners, Christ died for us. Much more then, having now been justified by His blood, we shall be saved from wrath through Him." Romans 5:8-9

2. The only thing we would add as a word of caution, is that while we agree with this statement of his in this section. He has already and will throughout this video, introduce a different way to contact the blood of Christ as opposed to what the New Testament teaches.

3. As stated before, it is the blood of Jesus Christ that saves, redeems, reconciles us and remits sin, but we have to let The Bible tell us how we contact that saving blood of Jesus. We have to let The Bible be the authority.

CLASS DISCUSSION: Did you agree/ like their arguments? Are there other passages you would have used?

Play Section 5 Arguments – 8:14-8:53

CLASS QUESTION: What argument/arguments did he make?

ARGUMENTS

1. He quotes the following passages.

2. Romans 6:23 "For the wages of sin is death, but the gift of God is eternal life in Christ Jesus our Lord."

3. Ephesians 2:8-9 "For by grace you have been saved through faith, and that not of yourselves; it is the gift of God, not of works, lest anyone should boast."

4. He then states as he has previously that a person must confess.

5. He then adds that a person must repent and turn from a sinful life and go the other direction.

CLASS QUESTION: How would you answer this? Do you agree?

AFTER DISCUSSION PLAY THE NEXT VIDEO SECTION.

Play Section 5 Response – 8:53-9:16

CLASS QUESTION: Did you agree with their response?

CLASS QUESTION: Would you have made any other arguments?

- Have the class discuss the response.

TEACHERS NOTES FOR DISCUSSION

1. Now, thirdly, he says that you must repent.

2. He is correct that repentance is required by God

   - Acts 17:30, Luke 13:3,5 mention the necessity of repentance

   - 2 Cor. 7:10 also defines repentance as "For godly sorrow produces repentance leading to salvation, not to be regretted; but the sorrow of the world produces death."

CLASS DISCUSSION: Did you agree/ like their arguments? Are there other passages you would have used?

Play Section 6 Arguments – 9:16-9:32

CLASS QUESTION: What argument/arguments did he make?

ARGUMENTS

1.   He references Romans 10:9 which says "that if you confess with your mouth the Lord Jesus and believe in your heart that God has raised Him from the dead, you will be saved. For with the heart one believes unto righteousness, and with the mouth confession is made unto salvation."

CLASS QUESTION: How would you answer this?

AFTER DISCUSSION PLAY THE NEXT VIDEO SECTION.

Play Section 6 Response – 9:32- 10:47

CLASS QUESTION: Did you agree with their response?

CLASS QUESTION: Would you have made any other arguments?

- Have the class discuss the response.

TEACHERS NOTES FOR DISCUSSION

1. We agree with Romans 10:9-10 because it is Scripture.

   • The problem with what he is doing

131

here thought is that he is mixing contexts.

- For instance, Romans 10:9-10 is Paul discussing what he wishes those unfaithful Jews would do to be saved. While, Romans is a letter written to Christians, if you look at the preceding context, Paul discusses in Romans 9:1-3 how he wishes he could be accursed for his Jewish brethren if it meant they could be saved. In Romans 10:1-4 he talks about how they had made their own righteousness and were ignorant of God's righteousness. He states what he wishes they would do to be saved.

- He is trying to make this a parallel passage with 1 John 1:9 which is written describing how Christians are to be saved by confessing their sins to God.

- Acts 8:13-22 is helpful in this situation because we can see the difference between initial salvation to become a Christian and how a Christian is forgiven of sins.

2. Notice also that this passage mentions only belief and confession, not repentance. Many times people will quote Romans 10:9-10 as what a person must do to be saved. They will state "there is no baptism in Romans 10:9-10". I always ask them if they must repent to be saved (Acts 17:30)? They always say yes.

I then say "but it's not in Romans 10:9-10?". They normally respond, "Yes, but it's in other passages so we know it's necessary." I then agree and say "Absolutely, baptism is in other passages as well so it doesn't need to be in Romans 10:9-10."

- Also note Romans 10:9-10 speaks of confessing Jesus Christ as Lord, not confessing our sins.

CLASS DISCUSSION: Did you agree/ like their arguments? Are there other passages you would have used?

Play Section 7 Arguments – 10:47- 11:39

CLASS QUESTION: What argument/arguments did he make?

ARGUMENTS

1. He begins this segment with "If you want to find Christ, he's as close as a prayer. And I want you to pray this prayer with me, right now...."

2. Then he proceeds to give what is called "The Sinner's Prayer"

CLASS QUESTION: How would you answer this?

AFTER DISCUSSION PLAY THE NEXT VIDEO SECTION.

Play Section 7 Response – 11:39-15:58

CLASS QUESTION: Did you agree with their response?

CLASS QUESTION: Would you have made any other arguments?

- Have the class discuss the response.

TEACHERS NOTES FOR DISCUSSION
It's important to ask a few questions as we examine his argument from this clip.

1. First, where did he get this prayer? Can we turn in our Bible, and show where to find this prayer or one like it?

   - We cannot because there is nothing like it is in Scripture. A person can use any Bible search engine, Google, etc. and they will not find a prayer like this in the New Testament.

2. Second, can we find an example of someone in the New Testament praying a prayer like this to become a Christian?

   - The Book of Acts is the book full of conversions. It is also the background for the books of Romans-Revelation.

   - After the church began in Acts 2, there are numerous accounts of people being saved, and NOT ONE of them was saved by saying a prayer.

   - Acts 2 – The People on Day of Pentecost

   - Acts 8 – The People of Samaria

   - Acts 8 – The Ethiopian Eunuch

   - Acts 9 – Saul

   - Acts 10 – Cornelius

- Acts 16 – Lydia
- Acts 16 – The Philippian Jailer
- Acts 18 – The Corinthians
- Acts 19 – The Ephesians

3. Thirdly, there is one example of a person in the Bible who was praying for salvation and did not receive salvation from his sins by praying. That person is Saul who becomes the Apostle Paul.

- Saul's conversion is discussed in Acts 9, 22, and 26.

- 1 Timothy 1:16 says that his conversion was a pattern for all those who would believe on Jesus Christ for eternal life

- As one reads the account of Saul meeting Jesus in Acts 9, he will notice that Paul meets Jesus and is obedient to Jesus's instruction. Paul then proceeds to fast and pray for 3 days in Damascus (Acts 9:9-11). However when Ananias meets Saul, he tells him something he must do to be saved (Acts 9:6,22:10). Ananias tells Paul, who had already prayed for 3 days, that he must "And now why are you waiting? Arise and be baptized, and wash away your sins, calling on the name of the Lord."

- If one is to be saved by praying a prayer, why wasn't Paul saved from his sins by praying? He even prayed for three days?

- The fact is that no one in Scripture was ever instructed to pray a prayer to be saved. Additionally, there are no examples of someone praying to become a Christian either.

CLASS DISCUSSION: Did you agree/ like their arguments?

- Are there other passages you would have used?

LESSON: **12**

EP. 5—THE SINNERS PRAYER?

Play Section 8 Arguments – 15:58-16:13

CLASS QUESTION: What argument/arguments did he make?

ARGUMENTS

1.   He says "In that simple prayer, you have stepped from darkness into light."

2.   He says "You have now identified with the family of the Lord, Jesus Christ."

CLASS QUESTION: How would you answer this?

AFTER DISCUSSION PLAY THE NEXT VIDEO SECTION.

Play Section 8 Response – 16:13-18:42

CLASS QUESTION: Did you agree with their response?

CLASS QUESTION: Would you have made any other arguments?

- Have the class discuss the response.

TEACHERS NOTES FOR DISCUSSION

1. A person does go from darkness to light (1 Peter 2:9) when they become a Christian, but not in the manner he described.

    - "But you are a chosen generation, a royal priesthood, a holy nation, His own special people, that you may proclaim the praises of Him who called you out of darkness into His marvelous light;" 1 Peter 2:9

    - Later in that same letter Peter wrote, 1 Peter 3:21

        a. "There is also an antitype which now saves us—baptism (not the removal of the filth of the flesh, but the answer of a good conscience toward God), through the resurrection of Jesus Christ"

    - Paul said similar thing to Ephesians in Eph. 5:8 and in Acts 26:18

        a. "For you were once darkness, but now you are light in the Lord. Walk as children of light" Eph. 5:8

    - In Acts 26:18, Paul connects turning from darkness to light to receiving forgiveness of sins

        a. "to open their eyes, in order to turn them from darkness to light, and from the power of Satan to God,

that they may receive forgiveness of sins and an inheritance among those who are sanctified by faith in Me.'" Acts 26:18

- When did that happen for Paul? Acts 22:16 arise and be baptized and wash away your sins, calling on the name of the Lord.

  a. Paul had prayed for 3 days prior to this and was still in his sins until he arose and was baptized and washed those sins away and in doing so Paul was calling on God's name in faith to save him (Col. 2:11-12, 1 Peter 3:21).

2. Then he says "You have now identified with the family of the Lord, Jesus Christ."

- The family of the Lord would be the body of Christ, the church

  a. Scripture calls the church

    i. Gal. 6:10 "the household of faith"

    ii. Eph 2:19 "household of God"

    iii. 1 Tim. 3:15 "but if I am delayed, I write so that you may know how you ought to conduct yourself in the house of God, which is the church of the living God, the pillar and ground of the truth."

    iv. Hebrews 12:23- "to the general assembly and church of the

firstborn *who are* registered in heaven"

- How does a person become a member of the Lord's family, the church?

  a. We are born into the family

     i. To those who believe, they have a right to become a child of God

        - John 1:12-13 "But as many as received Him, to them He gave the right to become children of God, to those who believe in His name: who were born, not of blood, nor of the will of the flesh, nor of the will of man, but of God."

     ii. They must be born again, not of the flesh, but of the Spirit

        - Jesus answered, "Most assuredly, I say to you, unless one is born of water and the Spirit, he cannot enter the kingdom of God. That which is born of the flesh is flesh, and that which is born of the Spirit is spirit." John 3:5-6

     iii. Those who are the sons of God are those who have been baptized into Christ and have put on Christ by faith

        - Galatians 3:26-27 "For you

are all sons of God through faith in Christ Jesus. For as many of you as were baptized into Christ have put on Christ"

iv. Salvation is in Christ and one gets into Christ by being baptized into Christ.

– "Therefore I endure all things for the sake of the elect, that they also may obtain the salvation which is in Christ Jesus with eternal glory" (2 Tim. 2:10).

CLASS DISCUSSION: Did you agree/ like their arguments? Are there other passages you would have used?

Play Section 9 Arguments – 18:42-18:47

CLASS QUESTION: What argument/arguments did he make?

ARGUMENTS

1. He says, "I encourage you to go to a Bible preaching church this Sunday."

CLASS QUESTION: How would you answer this?

AFTER DISCUSSION PLAY THE NEXT VIDEO SECTION.

Play Section 9 Response – 18:47-19:26

CLASS QUESTION: Did you agree with their response?

CLASS QUESTION: Would you have made any other arguments?

- Have the class discuss the response.

TEACHERS NOTES FOR DISCUSSION

1. Almost all churches claim to be Bible believing churches. What they mean by that is a totally different story.

2. The problem is that most churches don't teach the things of the Bible accurately, even though they believe it.

3. The church he attends for instance is a Bible believing church, but from this video we've seen they teach a different plan of salvation than Jesus and the apostles. He used many verses but left others out.

4. Jesus warned of false prophets in many passages

   - Matthew 7:15- "Beware of false prophets, who come to you in sheep's clothing, but inwardly they are ravenous wolves.

   - 1 John 4:1- "Beloved, do not believe every spirit, but test the spirits, whether they are of God; because many false prophets have gone out into the world."

   - Satan used Scripture in Matthew 4, he just used it out of content.

   - Some well-meaning human teachers will do the same thing

a. 2 Peter 3:16 "speaking in them of these things, in which are some things hard to understand, which untaught and unstable *people* twist to their own destruction, as *they do* also the rest of the Scriptures."

b. They are using Scripture, but twisting it, and their end is destruction for themselves and those who follow after them.

CLASS DISCUSSION: Did you agree/ like their arguments? Are there other passages you would have used?

Play Section 10 Arguments – 19:26-19:39

CLASS QUESTION: What argument/arguments did he make?

ARGUMENTS

1. He says "Go to a church where the preacher gets up and preaches from the Word of God.

2. A church where the preacher gives an altar call and gives people an opportunity to be saved."

CLASS QUESTION: How would you answer this?

AFTER DISCUSSION PLAY THE NEXT VIDEO SECTION.

Play Section 10 Response - 19:39- 20:30

CLASS QUESTION: Did you agree with their response?

CLASS QUESTION: Would you have made any other arguments?

- Have the class discuss the response.

TEACHERS NOTES FOR DISCUSSION

1. We obviously would agree your church should be a church where the preacher gets up and preaches from the Word of God.

2. As far as "a church where the preacher gives an altar call"

   - We do not agree with this.

   - An Altar call is the idea where people are invited down to "the altar" to pray the Sinner's prayer and give their lives to Christ.

   - This practice is noticeably absent from the New Testament.

   - The idea can be traced back to the 1700's where it originated with Charles Finney. In the 1800's, Dwight Moody, Billy Sunday, and Billy Graham made this a popular idea when they had arenas full of people and would invite thousands to come down to the front and "ask Lord Jesus to come into their heart."

3. In the Scriptures, people asked what to do to be saved and they were not told to pray a prayer.

   - They were told to believe in Jesus and

then taught what that meant which culminated in their belief, repentance, and baptism Acts 16:30-34.

- Those who believed already were told to repent and be baptized if they already believed Acts 2:38.

- Those who already believed, had repented, confessed, fasted and prayed were told to "Arise and be baptized and wash away their sins calling on the name of the Lord" Acts 22:16.

4. With respect, we would recommend that if you are at a church teaching you to pray a Sinner's prayer or ask Jesus into your heart, that you consider changing to a church that follows the Biblical plan of salvation.

CLASS DISCUSSION: Did you agree/ like their arguments? Are there other passages you would have used?

Play Section 11 Arguments - 20:30-20:40

CLASS QUESTION: What argument/arguments did he make?

ARGUMENTS

1. In this final segment, he says, "That's where you're hearing the gospel."

CLASS QUESTION: How would you answer this?

AFTER DISCUSSION PLAY THE NEXT VIDEO SECTION.

Play Section 11 Response - 20:40-End

CLASS QUESTION: Did you agree with their response?

CLASS QUESTION: Would you have made any other arguments?

- Have the class discuss the response.

TEACHERS NOTES FOR DISCUSSION

1. He says this after repeatedly offering a plan that is not in the gospel.

2. Gal. 1:8 warns of the danger of preaching something other than the Gospel that Paul preached in the New Testament and says, "But even if we, or an angel from heaven, preach any other gospel to you than what we have preached to you, let him be accursed."

3. We are supposed to preach the Truth in love and sometimes that includes telling others when what they teach does not line up with the Bible (Eph. 4:15).

4. This teaching of the Sinner's Prayer is not found in Scripture and is a man-made doctrine that we should correct because many people are misled by it.

5. Imagine being able to help correct someone teaching this so that they don't hear this on Judgement day.

   - Matthew 7:21-23 "Not everyone who says to Me, 'Lord, Lord,' shall enter the kingdom of heaven, but he who does

> the will of My Father in heaven. Many will say to Me in that day, 'Lord, Lord, have we not prophesied in Your name, cast out demons in Your name, and done many wonders in Your name?' And then I will declare to them, 'I never knew you; depart from Me, you who practice lawlessness!'

ADDITIONAL STUDY MATERIAL IF TIME PERMITS.

Many get the idea that we need to pray a prayer for salvation from passages like Romans 10:13 which says "For **whosoever** shall call upon the name of the Lord shall be saved."

- What does it mean to call upon the name of the Lord?

- Does it mean to pray for salvation?

- This phrase is found a few times in the New Testament.

- It is a quotation from the minor prophet Joel 2:32.

- It is found in Acts 2:21 and Romans 10:13

- In Acts 2:21 we are told "whoever calls on the name of the Lord shall be saved"

- How did the inspired apostle Peter interpret this statement?

  - He preached about the death, burial, and resurrection of Jesus and when those who heard ask what to do (to be saved) in Acts 2:37, Peter responded with "Repent and be

baptized everyone of you in the name of Jesus Christ for the forgiveness of your sins."

- The below chart shows the parallel.

Acts 2:21	Whoever	Calls	On the name of the Lord	Shall be saved
Acts 2:38	Everyone of you	Repent and be baptized	In the name of Jesus Christ	For the remission of sins

To further support this idea, in Acts 22:16 Paul had already been praying for 3 days and yet he apparently had not called upon the name of the Lord yet as Ananias said "arise and be baptized and wash away your sins, calling on the name of The Lord"

- If calling on the name of the Lord was praying a prayer then Paul would have already accomplished this many times during the previous 3 days in which he prayed (Acts 9:9-11)

- In Acts 22:16 the Greek word meaning call upon is "epikaleo".

  - This same word appears in Acts 25:11 where Paul "appealed" to Caesar or "called upon" Caesar.
  - 1 Peter 3:21 tells us that baptism is how we call upon or appeal to God through Jesus Christ

1. "Corresponding to that, baptism now saves you—not the removal of dirt from the flesh, but an appeal to God for a good conscience—through the resurrection of Jesus Christ." 1 Peter 3:21

If you or your students have any additional questions they would like answered, they are more than welcome to email Don and Aaron at **answeringtheerror@gbntv.org**

Tell the students that they can download the Gospel Broadcasting Network App to watch more episodes of Answering The Error and the many other programs that GBN has on their app and website www.GBNTV.org.

LESSON: **13**

WHAT MUST I DO TO BE SAVED?

This is a lesson to teach what a person must do to be saved. This is a good way to end the quarter.

What Does Someone Need to Do to Be Saved? Obeying the gospel can be summed up in 5 short words:

HEAR, BELIEVE, REPENT, CONFESS AND **BE BAPTIZED.**

1. First, a man must **HEAR** the gospel.

    a. He hears that because of his sin he has transgressed the will of God and is destined to die eternally in Hell.

        i. Romans 6:23 – "The wages of sin is death..."

    b. He hears also that Jesus Christ came as God in the flesh to pay the penalty for his sin....so that he won't have to.

    c. He hears that this salvation is found "IN" Christ.

        i. Romans 10:14 indicates that if one doesn't hear

the message of the gospel he has NO hope.

2. Upon hearing it, he must **BELIEVE** it. What does that entail?

   a. A man must understand that **Jesus is the Christ, the Son of God.**

      i. John 8:24, "Jesus said, "if ye believe not that I am he, ye shall die in your sins.""

   b. He must understand that He is Deity.

      i. John 1:14, " And the Word was made flesh, and dwelt among us, (and we beheld his glory, the glory as of the only begotten of the Father,) full of grace and truth."

   c. He must believe in the **Death, Burial, and Resurrection** of Christ.

   d. He must believe that while we were yet sinners Christ died for us (Rom. 5:8), and then arose defeating death (I Cor. 15:54-55)

      i. Romans 10:9, "that if you confess with your mouth the Lord Jesus and **believe** in your heart that God has **raised Him from the dead**, you will be saved."

   e. And it's crucial that a man believe and understand the body of Christ, which is the one church of the NT.

      i. 2 Tim. 2:10 says that salvation "in Christ."

    ii. Eph. 5:23 says Christ will save His body, the church (Eph. 1:22-23)

3. After believing, a person must **REPENT**.

    a. Acts 17:30 says, "Truly, these times of ignorance God overlooked, but now commands all men everywhere to repent..."

    b. Repentance is a change of mind, brought about by godly sorrow, that results in a reformation of life. 2 Cor. 7:10

4. A person must also be **WILLING TO CONFESS CHRIST**.

    a. Romans 10:10 clearly tell us, "For with the heart one believes unto righteousness, and with the mouth confession is made unto salvation....."

    b. In Acts chapter 8, as Philip was teaching the gospel to the Ethiopian, he said, "See, here is water; what hinders me from being baptized?"

        i. Philip responded, "If you believe with all your heart, you may." And he answered and said, "I believe that Jesus Christ is the Son of God" (Acts 8:37).

5. Finally, involved in obeying the gospel, one must **BE BAPTIZED**.

    a. Mark 16:16, Jesus said, "He who believes and **is baptized** will be saved; but he who does not believe will be condemned."

i. Baptism as practiced by first century Christians was total immersion.

ii. It is at this point that one contacts the saving blood of Jesus, and has "obeyed" the gospel.

01. Romans 6:3-4, "Or do you not know that as many of us as were baptized into Christ Jesus were baptized into His death? Therefore we were buried with Him through baptism into death, that just as Christ was raised from the dead by the glory of the Father, even so we also should walk in newness of life."

Once a person does these things, Acts 2:47 says the Lord will add you to THE church. Then the Christian grows and must be faithful unto death in order to receive a crown of life (Rev. 2:10).

Have you enjoyed this book? Would you like to teach more classes similar to the ones in this book? Below is a list of future books in this series along with their topics.

ANSWERING THE ERROR – BOOK 2

TOPICS:

1. What About-Same Sex Marriage? (2 Class Periods)

2. Do You Only Have to Just Believe? (2 Class Periods)

3. Should Christians Keep The Sabbath Day? (2 Class Periods)

4. Does the church of Christ Teach a Works Based Gospel? (4 Class Periods)

5. What is Purgatory and is it Biblical? (2 Class Periods)

ANSWERING THE ERROR – BOOK 3

TOPICS:

1. False Accusations of the Churches of Christ Part 1 (2 Class Periods)

2. False Accusations of the Churches of Christ Part 2 (2 Class Periods)

3. False Accusations of the Churches of Christ Part 3 (2 Class Periods)

4. False Accusations of the Churches of Christ Part 4 (2 Class Periods)

5. Where Did Satan Come From? (4 Class Periods)

ANSWERING THE ERROR – BOOK 4

TOPICS:

1. Is Jesus Really God? (2 Class Periods)

2. Do I Have to Be Baptized- In Depth Part 1 (2 Class Periods)

3. Do I Have to Be Baptized Advanced Part 2 (2 Class Periods)

4. Do I Have to Be Baptized Advanced Part 3 (2 Class Periods)

5. Do I Have to Be Baptized Advanced Part 4 (2 Class Periods)

"QR CODES"
FOR CLASS USE

Tear or cut these "QR Codes" out and tape or tack these "QR Codes" for class access. Announce to the class that the videos are available by scanning the "QR Code" for each lesson.

LESSON 1

LESSON 2

LESSON 3

LESSON 4

LESSON 5

LESSON 6

" **QR** CODES"
FOR CLASS USE

Tear or cut these "QR Codes" out and tape or tack these "QR Codes" for class access. Announce to the class that the videos are available by scanning the "QR Code" for each lesson.

LESSON 7	LESSON 8

LESSON 9	LESSON 10

LESSON 11	LESSON 12